DESERT AND THE CITY

Frère Ivan

DESERT AND THE CITY

A quest for interiority
in the footsteps of the Desert Fathers

Original title: *Désert et cité des hommes*
© Médiaspaul, Paris 1992

Translated by Rachel Orbell

Bible quotations herein are from the Revised Standard Version of the Bible, Catholic edition, copyright 1965 and 1966 by the Division of Christian Education of the National Council of the Churches of Christ in the USA, and are used by permission. All rights reserved.

Cover design by Mary Lou Winters based on the original by Françoise Ménétrier in 'Désert et cité des hommes'

ST PAULS
Middlegreen, Slough SL3 6BT, United Kingdom
Moyglare Road, Maynooth, Co. Kildare, Ireland

English translation © ST PAULS 1993

ISBN 085439 447 8

Produced in the EEC

Printed by The Guernsey Press Co. Ltd, Guernsey, C.I.

ST PAULS is an activity of the priests and brothers of the Society of St Paul who proclaim the Gospel through the media of social communication

Contents

Foreword	7
Introduction	9
1. Interiority and history	13
2. A broken world	23
3. At the centre of the world, human beings in the image of God	39
4. Human beings: the face of Christ	51
5. Silence, the way of truth	65
6. Solitude – desolation and blessing	83
7. The Eucharist, sacrament of our solitude	99
8. Prayer, the way of interiority	113

Foreword

Without being in the least 'autobiographical', these pages recount a personal spiritual experience, but one which has as its context the great tradition of the Church, and especially of the Desert Fathers. Whether it is due to the hundred of hermits currently living out their vocation, within the developments now sanctioned by Canon Law, or to other reasons, contemporary religious sensibility is rediscovering the riches of a tradition it has long forgotten or neglected.

More than a passing trend, the interest in this rediscovery lies in the fact that it opens up the possibility of a synthesis between two seemingly irreconcilable theological polarities: the vertical view, which emphasises divine transcendence, and the horizontal vision which finds God in human activity, and especially in the struggle for a more just society. A third path could surely be one which leads through the Desert, a quest for purification indispensable for the ever sinful and deluded human being, indispensable also for any real attempt to take charge of history. With this in view, some lines from the first chapter seem helpful in defining the author's quest:

The wisdom of the desert invites us first and foremost to overcome the evil within ourselves before we become involved in fighting evil in the world, and to drink from the living waters of the Gospel ourselves before we proclaim it to the world. The human heart is the focal point from which the transfiguration of history must take place, only the sanctified human being can sanctify the world. We are brought back to the words of Seraphim of Sarov: "Be at peace, and thousands around you will be saved."

Gerard Hoffbeck
Lecturer at the University of Strasbourg

Introduction

We live in a world 'full of sound and fury'. Not a week, a day or an hour goes by without bringing its share of wars, violence and indescribable suffering. Homicidal violence, especially war, seems to be one of the fundamental experiences of our history. In fact, the great 'stories' which are at the origins of the major civilisations and religions of the world are characterised by war: the Bible, the Koran, the Bhagavad Gita, the Iliad and the Greek tragedies, are full of the rumours of war.

Why is there this violence at the origins of history and throughout its course? According to philosophy, it is a dialectical necessity. But the Bible disagrees, since things were not like this in the beginning. The fratricidal conflict between Cain and Abel has a discernible basis: a spiritual defect, a law of death which we call sin. When St Paul cries: "For I do not do the good I want, but the evil I do not want is what I do" (Rom 7:19), he is expressing, in terms of an individual's experience, the tragic element in the history of universal humanity. Even today, humanity is producing deadly conflicts, monstrous acts of violence, intolerable injustice which it 'hates', but towards which it is helplessly drawn.

Where does this fascination with death arise? Whence this unbelievable capacity for hatred and destruction? From out of the 'black hole', the shadowy gulf hollowed out deep within each human being by their rejection of the Light. It is this dark area of violence to which theology gives the abstract name of sin. The gospels and the Desert Fathers talk in more concrete terms of 'tormenting demons'. Jung speaks of the 'Shadow' and modern psychopathology employs such ideas as perversion, complex and the death wish. This variety of symbols arising from the diversity of cultural backgrounds is an attempt to surround this mysterious and transcendent reality by the experience of what a perverted freedom, a congenital defect of the human mind is, without ever really managing to say it.

The victory of Light over darkness constitutes the whole venture of Christianity. In each individual human being, the light of truth and love must emerge slowly, opening up a way of freedom over and against the awesome pressures of the surrounding cosmos, over and against the powerful determinism of biology, and over and against the dramatic deviations caused by the lure of a shamefully egocentric pride and greed.

We know and believe that the tragedy of the human condition can be reversed, the human heart can be delivered from the Shadow which shrouds it, and can find peace in the silence of the Light. The eight chapters of this book describe this journey from the first great ruptures to the reconciliation found in the offering of the universal prayer of

Christ. The journey is a human one, that of every human being, and at the same time, that of all humanity contained in microcosm within that human being. My victory over the 'shadow' is that of all humanity, but my fall is a defeat for humanity. In the same way, the death of a person anywhere in the world hurts me, destroys me, kills me, myself, in humanity; but a loving gesture, a beautiful smile somewhere on the horizon, even unseen, gives me life, and makes my joy mysteriously complete.

We are one, together, in the Body of Christ, not as separate entities set side by side in some great container, but rather living in interpenetration, moving towards totality. Each person's story is that of all, for better or worse. This is why those who pray alone in the Desert, who live the reality of this communion in its intensity, can know themselves to be separated from all but united to all", deeply involved, co-responsible with all, in the one universal story which is human salvation. Whether one lives in the Desert or among the masses, co-responsibility in this task of salvation is the same for all. What distinguishes the Desert dwellers is that they show clearly, by their lives, the depth at which this struggle takes place: the very depths of the heart.

Finally, the Desert and the City are the settings for one and the same radical struggle – one that takes place at the very roots – to eradicate the cancerous 'shadow' from the human heart under the irridation of divine light. For this reason, words from the Desert can have a very real, if unexpected, relevance for the City.

Chapter 1
Interiority and history

"Those who drink of the water that I will give them will never be thirsty. The water that I will give will become in them a spring of water rushing up to eternal life" (Jn 4:14). Jesus' promise to the Samaritan woman is one which he makes to all. "Out of the believer's heart shall flow rivers of living water" (Jn 7:38). The Holy Spirit, flowing out in the water and blood from the heart of the crucified Christ, is given to us as a living spring, gushing up from the depths of our hearts, imparting to us the very life of God and transforming us little by little in his light. We must learn to discover this spring within ourselves and to drink from it, and so come ever nearer to the fullness of the divine life.

The Lord invites the Samaritan woman to become aware of this spring, to discover the wonderful lift which is offered to her. Like any of us, she is just a poor human being, very weak and unhappy, her life torn apart by sin: five men have in turn tried to create a fragile happiness with her but, too weak and unfaithful, they have disappeared, leaving her a little more bereft each time, subject to a frightening disintegration of her personality, having strayed still further from the source of real happiness.

We are each one of us this woman, and her story is that of all humanity. Her individual story bears the same ruptures as the history of humanity and reflects the same spiritual tragedy. It is to this woman, who can be identified with the whole of humanity, that the Lord shows a way to salvation she must descend to the depths of her heart and there draw from the living springs of salvation. She must discover the path to unity by the most intimate union possible with the One who is at the very roots of her being and life, the Spirit whose temples we are, as Paul assures us, and who comes to dwell in us. It is within us, in our interiority, that we discover our truth as human beings and the truth of God; it is there, where God reveals himself to us, no longer as an abstract idea, but as the great Living One, as the experience of life, as the one Reality. The paths of interiority alone can lead to this rich and vital experience.

What is history?

There has been so much speculation about this question by philosophers and theologians that one hesitates to add anything more. It appears that the relationship between history and interiority is similar to that between time and eternity, appearances and depth, phenomena and substance, matter and spirit. It is likely that history is nothing other than the present world in as much as it is the product of a past and full of potential for the future.

Product of an evolution with cosmic beginnings, this world is the setting and also the product of a human story which is unfolding according to a series of events in which we are the actors. We are making history. We are using our activity, our creativity in the task; our moral responsibility is involved. In other words, we are engaged in it; that is a matter of fact, whether we like it or not. Every move I make has world-wide repercussions. On the one hand it is partly conditioned by the past and, on the other hand, it opens up a future, it brings into being something which concerns not only me personally, but which will affect the whole of the human family, for good or ill. As Einstein's image put it: "I bang on my table and the echo reaches the nebula of Andromeda." He was speaking as a physicist, aware of the great laws of the cosmos, but it is even more true in the realm of human moral responsibility and the world of history in as much as human liberty brings it to be and shapes it by the decisions which make up our daily lives and preside over the great events of history.

We are responsible for each other to a degree which we find hard to imagine: each thought, each gesture has repercussions, sometimes imperceptible but sometimes important and easy to distinguish in all those who are spiritually close to us. This solidarity is far-reaching, extending to the whole mystical body of Christ which embraces the cosmos and the whole of the created world. It can truthfully be said that each one of us, in our own infinitesimal strength, is in charge of the whole world, is responsible for history, for his elements of tragedy as well as his brighter side.

On this understanding, to 'flee from the world', to escape from history, to withdraw from the contest by going to live in the Desert, to seek openly to break away from society in as radical a way as possible, like monks, living in the Desert: is this not to attempt the illegitimate and to go after an illusion, in that it is radically impossible to escape from one's responsibility as a human being, subject to temporality and involved, whatever the outcome, in the same common destiny with all humanity?

The monastic way, in fact, is seen as an attempt to disengage from the world, to be free from his value systems, judged as corrupt or at least insufficient, for the sake of another world, a world beyond the sparkle of deceptive appearances, in order to reach a certain truth, a source of light and joy, the source of eternal life hidden in the depths of the heart to which silence and solitude alone can lead.

It is an option for interiority. It involves in some way leaving the outside world, the superficial world of possessions and power, the world of appearances, in order to reach a deeper level of reality, a certain inner truth, the living spring of which Christ spoke to the Samaritan woman. "The kingdom of God has come near to you" (Lk 10:9). This is the kingdom to be reached by way of the 'inner life', to use an expression no longer fashionable today. This journey of interiority, this movement towards the depths of the heart, towards the secret place of God's dwelling, this descent towards the ultimate, this approach to the innermost being of a person who, as St Paul assures us, is the temple of the Holy Spirit, involves standing at a distance from any 'historical' engagement, a kind of rejection of history, in order to devote oneself entirely to a different kind of labour, a spiritual labour in which prayer, meditation, the intense struggle against sin, and the quest for purity of heart have first place.

At first sight, this option for interiority or interiorisation which is typically monastic and which sums up all that is meant by the monastic phrase 'flight into the desert' appears to be a rejection of history, an attempt to erase temporality completely in favour of eternity, an illusory effort to efface the tragedy of the human condition in the individualistic security of a purely interior bliss. And this criticism can be levelled not only at monks but at all Christians, in as far as they look for a hereafter or long for a peace and joy which they know only too well the world cannot give. They have the same tendency to live with their eyes fixed on heaven, instead of taking a courageous part in the harsh struggle for justice and peace in the City. An intensive spiritual quest for which one sacrifices everything else is easily seen as a way of opting out of the hard tasks imposed by life, which, for the majority of human beings, is little other than a hellish prison sentence.

This spiritual adventure leads us along the path of interiority in search of the living waters – and we must remember that these are the living waters of the Spirit flowing from the heart of Christ who died to save the world. But it does not turn us away from history, it does not make us strangers to the human family, it does not allow any lazy or selfish forgetfulness to efface the awesome questions posed by the destiny of humanity. Instead, it leads us gradually and ever more demandingly to the very heart of history, to the centre of all reality, to the centre of the world, right to the secret depths where the human heart is united with the heart of Christ, in whom and by whom are all things.

Here in this hidden, invisible place is worked out the salvation of the world. Here, in the innermost human heart, takes place the most radical, the most demanding, and sometimes the most agonising struggle to bring forth into the world a little innocence, a little joy and beauty. It is in the human heart, in the hearts of each of us, that after an intense struggle light triumphs over darkness, and the hatred which tears apart our world, the despair which destroys so many, the senseless pride and selfishness which are at the root of war, and the most terrible human suffering begin to recede.

The struggle for justice, involvement in society and the trade unions, the enormous political and diplomatic efforts to construct a world of peace and justice, the generosity of international solidarity in responding to many kinds of terrible suffering, are of course indispensable. But there is a kind of struggle which is even more urgent and more costly, because more radical, and which alone is effective since it occurs in the only place for which we have entire responsibility: our own heart. The salvation of the world is played out in the choices which are left to our human freedom. History and its long train of tragedies depend entirely on these radical choices for the light or the darkness, made in the very depths of every human consciousness.

"Be at peace, and thousands around you will be saved." St Seraphim of Sarov's words throw a particular light on the way in which we can take charge of history, by seeing history as merely the outward reflection of an interior in which human freedom is faced with the terrifying choice between good and evil. Everything comes from within the human heart. Jesus of Nazareth and his mother Mary understood this well, and set about the salvation of the world not by any political movement but by a sacrificial gift, willed from the very depths of the heart, so making certain the victory of love over hatred and death.

This is the journey which opens up before us: to descend to the depths of the heart and there discover, beyond the experience of death, the life which springs up for all eternity, and so to take charge of history and bring it to his fulfilment to the glory of the Father.

Everything takes place within, and it is essential to understand that the kingdom of God which Jesus tells us is 'within' us is one and the same thing as the kingdom which is to come at the end of time and which the Church, whose sole aim is to carry the Gospel to all the world, is seeking to establish. The wisdom of the Desert invites us first and foremost to overcome the evil within ourselves before we become involved with fighting evil in the world, and to drink of the living waters of the Gospel ourselves before we proclaim it to the world. The human heart is the focal point from which history must be transfigured; only the sanctified human being can sanctify the world. We are brought back to the words of Seraphim of Sarov: "Be at peace, and thousands around you will be saved".

Christian interiority

Is it possible to attempt a definition of what this involves? The question is relevant, since the major Eastern religions are today increasingly attractive to a growing number of people in the West; they too are held out as religions of interiority in the sense that they open up a way towards the Absolute, seen in terms of the ultimate human dimension, of the person's inner being, and accessible by means of meditation and the techniques of concentration and contemplation.

The sole aim of the Bible and of Judaeo-Christian revelation as a whole is to indicate the path which human beings are to follow in order to reach God. God and humanity, humanity and God: this one subject forms the basis of all religious teaching.

Two main types of image can be seen which seek to express the relationship between human beings and God: firstly images of exteriority, in which God is seen as the Most High, he who dwells in heaven. They are images of transcendence, conveying the absolute otherness of God. God is in the heights above, and in order to reach him, one must rise up, ascend Mount Sinai or Mount Tabor. One must leave self behind, leave one's country and one's people. The journey towards him involves relinquishing one thing after another, heading towards a far goal which is ever more distant. Or rather, it is a journey 'with' him, 'before' him, to fulfil his ever mysterious will and realise his plan of salvation for the world by as exact an obedience as possible.

But alongside these are other images based on interiority: God is seen as being within a person, speaking to the heart and making his dwelling there.

In the words of Hosea: "Therefore I will now allure her, and bring her into the wilderness, and speak tenderly to her" (Hos 2:14), or as we find in numerous passages of the New Testament, in both the gospels and the letters of St Paul: "...the kingdom of God has come to you" (Lk 11:20), "...your body is a temple of the Holy Spirit within you..." (1 Cor 6:19), "Abide in me as I abide in you... As the Father has loved me, so I have loved you; abide in my love" (Jn 15:4,9), "...my Father will love them, and we will come to them and make our home with them" (Jn 14:23) and especially in St Paul's well known words: "...it is no longer I who live, but it is Christ who lives in me" (Gal 2:20). The thrice Holy God, Father, Son and Holy Spirit, is present in person in the depths of the human heart, a spring creating and transfiguring in the light of divine grace.

Human salvation is found in this alone. Only God can save humanity by freeing our hopelessly tragic history from the domination of death and turning it into a holy history, a divine history. We have the greatest of difficulty in convincing ourselves of one truth, which is that all the wrongs, all the disasters which even today are tearing our humanity apart, have a directly spiritual cause. There is no war, no racial hatred, no social conflict, no violence of any kind, nor any famine or devastating epidemic whose origin cannot be found in the senseless choice of human liberty which prefers death to life, hatred to love, contempt for God to humble submission to his wisdom. This is what we are taught explicitly in the first pages of Genesis. If this world which was once a paradise has become hell, it is because human beings wanted it so, and still do.

Cardinal Lustiger has reminded us clearly that the basic problem of humanity and history is a religious problem, a problem found at the roots of the human psyches, this secret gulf, almost unknown to human beings themselves, in which their liberty, responding to God with a yes or a no, opens up the way to life and love or else, in rebellious pride, chooses death.

Thus we can see how close is the connection between history and interiority. The long drama of human history, with its play of shadows and light, is no other than the drama of interiority, the willingness to open to the light or the rejection of it; it is the drama of the Spirit which, after many failures and rejections, gradually rouses, draws and moves each human consciousness by means of its own deepest spontaneity, uniting all in one divine communion, the Mystical Body which fills the universe.

Those who live in the Desert, then, far from leading an unnaturally marginalised existence at the edges of history, are instead involved at its heart, at the cutting edge of the famous 'struggle for humanity' on which depends the emergence of that 'new humanity' capable of building the City of God in peace and solidarity. The silence of the Desert – and is not every human heart a 'desert'? – is the setting for the most severe and difficult 'human struggle', one which alone is decisive, since it aims to conquer hatred and death in the furthest reaches of the human consciousness itself, so preparing a way to its transfiguration in the peace of the Holy Spirit and to the transfiguration of the whole human family.

Chapter 2
A broken world

The setting for our spiritual adventure, and that of all humanity as it, too, searches for the living waters, is a broken, divided world, doomed to tragedy and death. But we cannot simply call it the 'setting', since the world and history, far from being a mere backdrop, are themselves the substance of the adventure in which we are involved. This adventure is shared even by the Word of God, who was willing to descend to the darkest depths of our human condition in order to enlighten us, to transform us inwardly, and to offer us up to the Father.

We cannot help but look on the world of today, not so much with pessimism, since pessimism has to do with a future which eludes us, but with anguish. All the great minds of our time, philosophers and writers from Solzhenitsyn to Elie Wiesel, hold out to us the image of a world of chaos, horribly torn apart. Music and the plastic arts rely on techniques of rupture, discords which remain unresolved and violent rhythms which in their intensity are a perfect representation of a chaos which refuses to be assuaged by wisdom and harmony. Against a background of such gloom, the messages of ultimate hope repeated by the Pope or by Mother Teresa take on an even greater intensity. Our era seems to bear the mark of tragedy – to a greater degree than other periods of history? It is hard to say, since this age shows us that without a single exception, every nation, every civilisation on every continent, has lived through an incredible series of catastrophes, wars and unbelievably destructive violence. But the speed and efficiency of communication today mean that each individual citizen on the earth is made conscious of virtually all the suffering taking place in the world. Today it is not only the occasional neighbourhood beggar who knocks on our door in need, but all humanity.

Perhaps this explains why so many people today are crushed and oppressed by a feeling of insurmountable tragedy. We are aware of something terrible or, to be more precise, of something evil in the human condition. Whether we like it or not, we are deeply affected by this atmosphere of tragedy, which has transformed the earth from a paradise created by God into a living hell for the majority of the five billion people who currently make up the world's population.

There are two main lines of thought about the causes of this disastrous situation. The first sees wars, increasing violence and the crises which are tearing apart humanity, as a necessary stage in an evolution which, like that of any species of animal, is subject to the law of the struggle for life. It ensures the survival of the fittest and best adapted, and brings about progress in a way which is beneficial to all the inhabitants of the globe. The setbacks and the dreadful suffering of which we are aware, are seen merely in terms of the scale of observation, or as a percentage on the debit side. All that affects humanity in a negative way is seen simply in terms of 'mistakes', never exceeding the quotas which are, after all, reasonable enough. Such is the optimistic view of a supposedly scientific version of evolution, reminiscent of Marx, or, to some extent, even Teilhard.

The Bible teaches us something quite different. The beauty and harmony of the world which God created have been dramatically displaced by a catastrophic rupture for which no lasting and effective remedy can be found. In spite of huge efforts on the part of thousands, indicative of a good will which sometimes borders on the heroic, human beings are unable to rise above the disorder and corruption which seem to be an intrinsic part of our historical condition.

The world and humanity are burdened by a kind of fatality to which theologians have given the name 'original sin'. It is a fairly abstract notion which attempts to summarise the various richly symbolic and complex elements found in the first pages of the book of Genesis. Original sin is described as a wound, affecting a person's most intimate centre: their heart, their liberty. It brings with it corruption and death, as St Paul explains. Thus the Bible places human liberty at the origins of the drama of history, presenting that liberty in terms of the source of a choice, or a series of catastrophic choices. What was created a paradise has become hell through the free decision of human beings. They have chosen death and continue to make that choice; they have preferred rebellion and hatred to love and life.

As a result, the only means of alleviating the immense distress experienced by ourselves and all human beings is to change, to be converted, to free the human heart from the way of violence, pride and the need to dominate and possess. The solution to our tragedy is therefore to be found within the human heart. It is a solution which is far beyond our strength and demands nothing less than divine intervention.

The beginnings of history

The authors of the book of Genesis have attempted to solve the enigma of our human condition by offering to us, in the form of 'wisdom writings', an account of creation and of the first adventures of human beings. It provides us with one of the most extraordinary pages of literature in the world. It is the most profound attempt ever undertaken to provide, or at least suggest, veiled in the language of symbols, an explanation of the meaning of human life and the reasons behind the enormous difficulties which human beings encounter in their efforts to realise their own destinies and find fulfilment.

Every philosophy and every religion tries to find answers to these radical and vital questions. Indeed very recently, Fr Martelet has ventured to write a commentary on this extraordinary passage, and to respond to the eternal question: why evil, why suffering?

"In the day that the Lord God made the earth and the heavens, when no plant of the field was yet in the earth and no herb of the field had yet sprung up... then the Lord God formed man from the dust of the ground, and breathed into his nostrils the breath of life; and the man became a living being" (Gen 2:4-5,7).

Here humans are seen as being at the summit and centre of the universe, the epitome of all that has preceded them. They are at the highest point of a great upward sweep. They blossom as a fulfilment, giving sense to all that has gone before; but they are destined to lead the way to something new, having received in their nostrils the mysterious breath of God. Herein lies the tragedy; human beings are born of the earth, fashioned from the clay in the same way as every other animal, yet they bear themselves a 'breath' which comes from God and which destines them to some greater end. It is the breath of the spirit, the breath of the freedom of a consciousness open to the infinity of God. Created free beings, humans are called into a communion with God, to attain to the supremely spiritual condition of friendship with God, sharing in his life and in his divine nature itself.

A kind of inner heaviness draws human beings downwards to fulfil the selfish demands of their animal nature. But at the same time there exists within them a strong, upward urge towards freedom from self, arising from that liberty which is called to move towards God and to prove itself more and more to be the means to communion with God. Thus, from the outset, human beings are divided and torn apart within, reaching out towards a destiny which is only realised in a very hazardous way, since it is dependent on their freedom. And that destiny proves to be extremely fragile: both yes and no are possible, but freedom very often chooses to say no.

The well-known story of the temptation tries to make accessible the drama of human liberty: "Now the serpent was more crafty than any other wild animal that the Lord God had made. He said to the woman, 'Did God say, "You shall not eat from any tree in the garden"?'..." (Gen 3:1). In this instant occurs that great rupture which brought about the dichotomy within human beings, and which was to lead to the deep-rooted disintegration of the personality described by St Paul at the other end of the Bible: "For I do not do the good I want, but the evil I do not want is what I do" (Rom 7:19). From this moment on, human beings have lost their inner unity, and have become the wretched, disjointed beings whose weakness we experience daily.

This first lapse is presented in terms of the breaking of a divine law: Eve eats the forbidden fruit, an act of material disobedience similar to those with which we are familiar. But the passage provides a much deeper analysis. Before the material act of disobedience there was a decision, a choice which is of much greater import. It is a properly spiritual sin like that of the angels: a sin of pride. Satan had in fact given Eve this hope: "...you will be like God, knowing good and evil" (Gen 3:5). This is spiritual pride, the pride of the spirit pure and simple: human beings refuse to accept another's laws, claiming the right to govern themselves and to decide what is good or bad, insisting on complete freedom from God. The Bible shows clearly that at the root of every wrong can be found pride, the pride of the spirit which refuses to recognise anyone greater than itself and will not submit in humble, loving obedience.

It is very striking to note that for all its variety, intelligence and structured thought, the atheism of today which has made famous the greatest names in philosophy, has practically only one theme: the 'liberation' of human beings: their liberation from God in an attempt to ensure their own greatness at God's expense, and the 'death of God' so that they might live. We have here the source of the most radical perversion of the human mind: God is love, he is totally giving and loves human beings enough to die for us, but in our pride and with the help of the prince of lies – as the passage suggests – we make a parody of him, turning him into a tyrant who denies our liberty and destroys our personality by his moralizing demands.

Satan is seen as playing a leading role in this perversion of the human intelligence. It is he who suggests that the divine law against eating the fruit of the tree of life is a plot devised by God to prevent human beings from being like him, "knowing good and evil" (Gen 3:4). It is he who presents God as a rival to human beings, a despot, seeking to retain his superiority over human beings by every means at his disposal. God becomes an evil being, a tyrant whose power can and must be destroyed. We are reminded of Voltaire's phrase: "Stamp out abuses", or of Nietzsche's "Laughing prophet", and the terrifying mockery behind his words "God is dead". Or again, there is the sheer violence of the sense of liberty found in the writings of Sartre, which brings him to a belief that "if God exists, humanity does not", since he sees divine omnipotence as the absolute contradiction of any kind of human liberty.

All this enables us to understand the truly spiritual roots of the drama of humanity. It is the drama of a liberty which is in thrall to pride because of its misguided demand for autonomy, personal greatness and self-worship. This demand leads to a spiritual rebellion, expressed in the concrete, material refusal to obey laws established by a transcendent wisdom. At the root of all sin is spiritual pride, unconscious, implicit and hidden, but which reveals itself as the original source of the rupture between humanity and God and, in consequence, as the most formidable factor in the disintegration of the human personality.

By choosing to follow their own laws, human beings find themselves not under a law of wisdom and reason, but subject to the complete anarchy of all the impulses which they are unable to control. Having rebelled and broken away from the deepest source of their being and life, humans are thrown into a whirling, destructive chaos which leads to that total loss of 'sense' which St Paul described so feelingly in the passage quoted above.

This first great rupture, the most radical of all, which cuts off human beings from their own depths and from their divine source, is to be followed by several others which finally make our world into a 'broken' world, doomed to tragedy and death. The Bible describes in great detail the origins of the important ruptures found throughout our history. The second of these ruptures concerns the first couple: Adam separates from Eve. In the biblical narrative he distances himself from her by an accusation: "The woman whom you gave to be with me, she gave me the fruit from the tree, and I ate" (Gen 3:12). She who was bone of his bone, flesh of his flesh, with whom he had lived in the transparency of perfect communion, has been made into an object, a stranger, a temptress, the accomplice of the great Adversary. A rift has appeared between the two; self-interest has resulted in the erection of barriers, illustrated by the wearing of clothes to defend a modesty until then unknown. Shame, in the form of a rejection of mutual transparency, and the awareness of a vague feeling of guilt, has underlined the disunity of the couple.

This was the beginning of the male-female dialectic which continues even today along the lines of the master-slave dialectic analysed by Hegel: dominator-dominated, owner-owned, a dialectic between beings who have been reduced to objects, which rarely results in communion and dialogue between real subjects who acknowledge their mutual otherness. Henceforth, women become objects to be possessed by men, and men by women, objects of seduction and domination, sometimes degraded even to the point of losing any human identity or confronted as enemies in conflicts which break out in deadly hatred and contempt.

This is how the Bible describes the failure and perversion of the human 'eros'. Sexuality which is in itself such a beautiful and creative force, a force which can open into communion with another, can be perverted into a terrible and bitter selfishness. Instead of "love of others to the point of self contempt", which is how St Augustine defines charity – charity being one and the same things as eros, desire for another in its highest, spiritual degree – we find "love of self to the point of contempt for others", a contempt which leads to others being treated simply as objects to be possessed and exploited. The rejection of communion, the rupture between men and women, the inability to live in genuine intersubjectivity are the root causes of the various perversions of sexuality to be found all too easily in our corrupt Western world. The shameful trade in prostitution and the unbridled spread of eroticism in all its forms illustrate a state of imbalance, the almost total disintegration of the vital forces of the human personality. At the root of this is the way in which Adam sees. He looks at Eve and no longer recognises in her the bone of his bone and flesh of his flesh, but sees her instead as a stranger, an 'object' to be feared, hated or possessed.

The third great rupture described in Genesis is of the ties of human kinship: Cain kills Abel. The deep-seated rift between man, Adam, and woman, Eve, initiates a new mode of existence for humanity which is no longer one of communion but of juxtaposition and opposition. The failure of human eros in the realm of conjugality is matched by a failure in the realm of kinship. Desire for the 'other', and for an encounter with that other in the communion of love or friendship, is perverted into hatred. Here too, it is the way we see which is important. Our gaze no longer has that transparency needed in order to reach another person in their true beauty, in the wonder of a subjectivity which is completely new and inalienable. Instead, we see no further than the narrow confines of our selfishness and fear. Individuals see only themselves, reality is perceived only through the distorting mirror of their longings for power and domination. In these circumstances, the other becomes an enemy, an opponent to be destroyed. Thus Cain kills his brother Abel. The first murder in history sets in motion a spiral of violence: Lamech demands seventy-sevenfold vengeance. One human being has become capable not only of killing another but of putting to death their family, their tribe, their entire race if necessary. Lamech is the forerunner of Auschwitz.

The deadly violence which has torn apart the world for thousands of years is a hellish perversion of a love which is its equal in depth and intensity. Hatred is merely the inversion of love in the heart of human beings who are made, as we know, in the image of a God who is love. The work of the crucified Word of God is to reclaim for love the powerful drive which has been inverted into hatred: to change hatred into love. What is involved, in fact, is a new creation. Human beings have become mutual enemies. The solidarity of the human family has been broken. So-called conventional or atomic wars, revolutions, riots, terrorism, government by means of widespread torture, concentration camps and re-education camps, genocide and ethnocide (two words invented recently to name crimes previously unknown) are just some of the faces of hatred in today's world.

A less violent kind of hatred between human beings, but one which is just as destructive to the true face of humanity, is slavery, the 'exploitation of one human being by another'. In the armed conflicts of the past, the enemy was either killed in combat or taken prisoner and sold as a slave. A slave is no more than an animal exploited for its ability to work, an animal which is only allowed sufficient leisure to recover its strength in order to maintain a reasonable return, and whose salary or its equivalent, is kept at the minimum required to ensure its survival and renewal by means of the birth of offspring destined to replace it when old age has rendered it useless... This is, in summary, Marx's description of the conditions of the working class last century, and it remains perfectly valid for a significant number of the world's population today. 'The exploitation of one human being by another' is still one of the great evils in our world. Everywhere the weak are oppressed by the strong, whether imperial nations, the 'nobles', or so-called favoured social classes, not necessarily labelled by any 'nomenclature', or even the most gifted or most devious individuals within a social group.

Violence and injustice seem to be so much a part of the fabric of history that there is little we can do in the face of this law of the strongest, this violence, found on all levels from international relations to social structures and individuals.

The book of Genesis records another great rupture, one which affects the harmony of the cosmos. "Cursed be the ground because of you..." (Gen 3:17) is the divine malediction, and St Paul talks of creation as being "in bondage to decay" (Rom 8:21). Human beings were meant to rule over the world and over the animals. This is indicated in the biblical narrative by the names which are given them, to identify their species, of course, but above all to show the 'knowledge', or in other words, the understanding, the respect, the friendly interest which human beings have for the animal kingdom which they govern. Human beings were meant to take their place within the harmony of creation, the 'cosmos', an organised whole, a unity made in beauty by divine wisdom. Human beings have given names to the animals, and also to the plants, minerals, stars and, recently, to 'alpha' and 'gamma' rays, and to the hundreds of atomic or subatomic particles discovered in the course of this century, thus extending their power over the world. Such knowledge, usually marked by admiration and friendship, is in fact a recognition of our common origin, our roots in the one fabric of matter and energy which bond us closely together with the whole of the cosmos. This knowledge of the world should blossom into celebration, joy and worship, but nearly always it is perverted into violent conquest, in order to satisfy an increasingly destructive desire for power and domination. Human beings have in fact begun to destroy the world, to consume and exploit it, to enslave it to their corrupt desire for domination. They are yielding to an intoxication with power which is leading to destruction and against which the ecological movement has rightly arisen.

The frightening extension of human power over nature, due to techniques and instruments of increasing skill and sophistication, has created in many people today a kind of 'technological' mania which seems to be one of the most pernicious idolatries of our time. Human beings can do anything: land on the moon, construct life artificially, create new species of plants, animals and perhaps even human beings before too long. Genetic engineering, governing the natural characteristics of any given species is already in operation. Science and technology, wonderful in themselves, can result in a genuine craze, which constitutes a great spiritual danger: human beings become totally absorbed in the conquest, they no longer see things in perspective and lose their critical faculties; their spiritual horizons are blocked by the extraordinary powers, riches and knowledge they have amassed, and they prove to be completely incapable of regulating the use of them, witness the present confusion caused by the question of artificial insemination.

As a conclusion to this brief survey of the human condition, both present and perennial, as it is interpreted in the Bible, we can say that our one task is to try to 'heal' these ruptures, to restore the world to unity and solidarity, to a communion which will incorporate all matter in a kind of huge, cosmic act of worship, turning the created universe, material as well as spiritual, into one long Eucharist to the glory of the Father.

The one thing which human beings must do is to rediscover their own depths, to find in divine transcendence the ultimate dimension of their being and, thence, absolute Immanence itself. Human beings have lost touch with the centre which is 'nearer to them than they are themselves', the source of all goodness, all beauty and all love. Thrown outside themselves by the diversity and confusion of their passions and instincts, they have lost their 'inwardness', that integral subjectivity in which their liberty is confirmed as a gift drawing them as children to the Father. This 'inwardness' must be rediscovered at all costs, since it is the source of all the blessings and happiness in human life. The dramatic and disastrous deviations of history have been due entirely to the obliteration or eradication of interiority from the human heart. Whence the absolute urgency of a return to the spring deep within which, as Christ promised the Samaritan woman, will "gush up to eternal life" (Jn 4:14).

Chapter 3
At the centre of the world, human beings in the image of God

How is unity to be restored to this broken world, torn apart by sin and doomed to death? How can limits be imposed on the violence and injustice which flourish on every side? How can wisdom and peace, true heralds of the kingdom of God, replace the meaninglessness and madness which seem to have become the rule in human behaviour? How can we return to the Paradise from which we have been excluded, and to the original harmony which God desires for his creation?

We have seen the answer: human beings are the key to creation, the direction marker, the focal point of a cosmic and biological process of maturation. They are its end result and they summarize each of its major stages in the unity of their corporal and spiritual make up. The human being is a 'microcosm', a world in miniature which incorporates all the component parts of the universe. They are true 'homing devices', but we have seen how far they have strayed from the intended trajectory, draggling all creation with them in a long, drawn out catastrophe. The dramatic change of course has its origins in a free decision, brought about by the enticement of the serpent who lured human beings far away from the living springs of wisdom and love. Since the tragedy was brought to its culmination in the human consciousness or heart, it is there, too, where the solution must be found. Everything depends on a change of heart, a conversion which will make it once again the temple of the Holy Spirit, where the kingdom of God can come, the kingdom which the Lord tells us in the gospels is upon us.

The kingdom of God is in fact first of all an inner, personal reality. It is God's in-dwelling, the opening up of a space in the human consciousness in which the Spirit of God can set forth the splendours of life and love, establishing a communion among human beings which forms them into the one Mystical Body of Christ. At the end of time, the looked-for kingdom will be no other than the completion of this immense task of the in-gathering of all creation in Christ, at the hour when, as St Paul says, he will hand over all things to his Father: the end of the world, the completion of history.

It is all one and the same activity, whether we are intent on the kingdom within, passionately searching for the living waters of the Spirit, or working for the coming of the kingdom on earth. The two kingdoms are in fact one, although many people separate them as if human interests were quite other than the interests of God. Only God's concern enables us to have a genuine concern for others, and to share with them a truly human life. How are we to give of the living waters, if we ourselves do not have access to the spring? We must first drink from the spring, enter the kingdom within, and then and only then, extend this kingdom around us. Nevertheless, the dialectic between the two kingdoms remains unresolved and they are only fully identified at the end of our life: if we are working to further the kingdom around us, we are thrust more deeply into the reality of the kingdom within. The apostolic task not only manifests but also creates and demands an ever deeper conversion.

The human vocation

Let us take a passage from Origen as our guide. "Each soul contains a well of living water, in which is hidden the image of God. The opposing powers have choked this well with earth. But now that Christ has come, let us dig out our wells, rid them of earth, and clear them of all debris. We will find living water there, that water of which the Lord says: 'If you believe in me, streams of living water will flow from your heart'" (Homily on Genesis, 1-4).

Here we find an important statement: human beings are made in the image of God. On reflection, that is a surprising, even staggering, assertion, since our everyday experience provides a rather poor view of human beings with their wretched bodies, their limitations, their failures and perversions. It seems far-fetched to think that in looking at a human being we can gain an idea of what God is, in his mystery, his infinity, and his eternity.

We are all familiar with Voltaire's sarcastic remark: "If God created us in his own image, we have more than reciprocated!" The words are intended to raise a smile, but perhaps they contain a deeper truth: God and humanity are related, and how we talk about God affects the way we talk about ourselves and vice versa. Our image of human beings, their destiny, the fulfilment they are to attain, the moral laws they must obey: all these are the substance from which we construct our theology. How we talk about God is a fairly accurate reflection of the way we experience ourselves. The rightness of what we say about either, which may always of course increase, can be seen to be directly dependent on the deepening of our spiritual experience. What we say about God is determined by what we have discovered, but what we discover depends on who we are and how the discovery is made. The discovery of God, the leap into his mystery, transforms us even as it is happening. Thus what we say concerning God is a fairly accurate reflection of who we are, and how we talk about God to others inevitably reveals our personality. Voltaire was right: we make God in our image, and this image is often a dangerous and wretched caricature, opposed quite understandably by various forms of atheism. The God of such and such a thinker or such and such a theologian, or of each one of us, is often no more than the rough outline of an easily restored original, or the projection of an entirely human personality, still far removed from any real identification with its divine model.

The discovery that human beings project their own personalities onto the image they make of God, helps us in our exploration of the full depths of the biblical statement that we are made in the image and likeness of God. Such a statement expresses a deep intuition, and at the same time, a rich promise. It is an intuition that human beings carry within themselves a divine spark, a secret and glorious dimension which can be termed nothing other than divine, a deep, hollow emptiness which opens into infinity. Human beings are not God: that is only too clear; they are merely creatures, limited and fragile indeed, but possessing an element of divinity, a 'something' which allies them to God and makes them fundamentally different from all other creatures. Because of it they defy our powers of intellect and analysis, acquiring a certain air of mystery, a vague, indefinable aura which eludes our understanding, like God himself. It is this 'something' which the Bible calls 'image'.

When we talk about the image of God in human beings, we are expressing the idea that "humanity is infinitely greater than humanly", that human beings contain a kind of 'absolute', valuable in its own right, independent of and unaffected by any reference to the rest of the world. In one whole aspect of their being, humans are free of the world of scientific causality which tries to explain all that exists by converging series of determinisms. To a certain degree human beings transcend the various pressures and impulses which burden them and they are able to excercise a kind of divine sovereignty. In other words, they can act 'freely'.

Whereas the behavioural patterns of other creatures, and of living beings in particular, are entirely determined by the laws of physics or biology, human beings are able to accomplish certain actions in complete freedom and creativity. A spontaneous action constitutes an absolute beginning, inexplicable by any cause but itself. It is the product of a truly creative power which is capable of bringing about something radically new in the realm of love, of life or of beauty. A spontaneous act of kindness brings into existence something essentially new: where there was once nothing, life and love spring forth in an abundance which defies all pre-planning and contrivance. In just the same way, an unkind action is destructive, it introduces a void into creation where nothingness and death blot out being and life. It is an act of 'dis-creation'. The power to create or 'dis-create', the power to be (to some extent) the absolute origin of an action, belongs to human beings alone.

Human beings are thus a source of grace and of gratuity in the world. God is gracious and gives freely, and that which comes closest in human beings to the generous, overflowing kindness and beauty which characterise the divine being and which are conveyed by the words grace or gratuity, is, precisely, liberty. This liberty is the glorious possibility of being the virtually absolute origin of life and love, a liberty unconstrained by the inexorable mechanisms of nature, whose remarkable perfection and extreme delicacy can be reproduced almost as well by robots. What makes human beings infinitely more than robots or highly evolved animals is freedom. Freedom is a divine spring, a divine potential for gratuity. It then becomes clear why this radical, essential freedom is seen as the greatest human privilege, the basis of personal dignity, and an indication that within the human being there exists an impenetrable unknown, a mysterious depth which we are unable to fathom by intellectual analysis and which is comparable to the mystery of God alone. God is personal, tri-personal in fact, and in the same way, the human being is a person, an absolute, a focal point of decision and love, with a potential for giving and being open to communion with others.

To say of human beings that they are persons, is to refuse to see in them merely individuals, 'individualised substances', enclosed within the narrow confines of their own being, existing only in themselves and for themselves. It is instead, to affirm that they possess the potential for openness, acceptance, and communion with others, entirely respectful of differences, in a style of relationship modelled on the Trinity. The Persons of the Trinity live in the closest possible unity while respecting the differences which distinguish them. Each of the Persons remains entirely themselves and yet, far from being simply juxtaposed or in conflict, they live in intimacy, communion and the most perfect mutual love. When we claim that human beings are persons created in the image of God, we are presented with a model not only for relationships between families and spouses, but also for social relationships. This model is the mysterious generosity of divine 'poverty' which is at one and the same time the utter emptying of self, and plenitude. It is a model which contains the nucleus of a whole philosophy and theology of human relationships, particularly of marriage, and even a complete social policy.

From image to icon

"God created humankind in his image" (Gen 1:27). We are dealing here not only with an intuition of what human beings are, but with the promise of what they are to become, a perception of their noble destiny. The Bible gives us an image of human beings which is sometimes harsh, even brutal and certainly dramatic in its realism. But the description of their fall is relieved by a thread of hope, a whisper, a call to greatness, a reaching out towards the heights of sanctity unique in the history of civilisation, and capable of satisfying the very highest of human aspirations.

Human beings, created in the image of God, are to attain to his perfect likeness. The biblical passage does not appear to make any distinction between the two words which are simply a repetition of the same idea. But Tradition has placed a very strong emphasis on the difference between them, setting them at opposite extremes of the human story which stretches from the beginning of the world until the end of time. To begin with, human beings are created in the image of God, but the image is deeply marred by sin; it is partially destroyed, broken apart by the huge ruptures described above. But at the end of history, and at the end of our individual journeys, we will be perfect beings, bathed in divine light, who have rediscovered their inner truth, their ultimate identity as children of God, able to receive, each according to their own capacity, the fullness of the divine life, and so become 'like' God.

The New Testament clarifies and completes the intuitions given in the passage from Genesis by emphasising the fatherhood of God, and the fact that we resemble him in the way that children resemble their parents. Thus the ideal way of life which Jesus holds out to us is summed up in his invitation to us to "be perfect... as your heavenly Father is perfect" (Mt 5:48). This is the design inherent in our personality: to become transparent to the perfect face of merciful Love within us. The Son is the image of the Father, "the reflection of God's glory and the exact imprint of God's very being" (Heb 1:3). Christ, who is God made human, is the model and the perfect example of a humanity made divine. In him and through him, the merciful Love which brought us into being takes complete possession of us.

To begin with, our freedom is like a seed buried in the mud of sin or, as Origen put it, like a living spring at the bottom of a well blocked with debris. In our freedom, we are destined to pass through various difficulties, through suffering and death, to bring to its fullest possible realisation the image we bear within us, so that we might become icons of the divine glory, sacred images in which God's holiness is reflected. It is God's holiness, given individual expression, which we contemplate in the faces of the saints. Reconciled by the Wisdom of God, radiant with his goodness, they communicate to us the mystery of God, each one revealing to us just one of the infinite variety of aspects of the unique, unseen Face. For although they are no more than the tiniest of mirrors, minutely resembling this face, yet the face of every saint reflects the shining immensity of infinity.

Perfect resemblance, which follows our transfiguration in the light, will not be attained until the last day. It is the fruit of a lifetime's labour, a work of art slowly fashioned by the gradual penetration of grace into the sinful heart and body with which we begin.

But it is not only individual human beings who are called to live by the gift of the Spirit and become icons of God. Humanity as a whole, unified, reconciled and transformed into the Body of Christ, the Body of the Word of God, is to become a perfect icon, a pure ray of divine glory and holiness. The communion of many human beings in the unity of the one Body, will then be a wonderful reflection of the consubstantial Trinity, the unity of three Persons in one divine essence. From Adam to the last of the righteous at the end of the age and including each one of the five billion people alive today, all human beings are called to live in unity and solidarity amidst the glory of a creation radiant with the brightness of a face.

A transfigured world

We now have the key which allows us to interpret the mystery of our personality and our destiny. We are able to see more fully the truth about each other, and so to understand the noble yet tragic secret carried in the intimate depths of another's heart. We can look at the forgotten beggar we pass in the street, the Peruvian Indian or the Chinese woman whose photograph we are shown, and know for certain that they are images of God, that God is their Father, that we are children together, born of one love; that they are bone of our bone, flesh of our flesh, and that the blood of kinship flows in our veins. When we say this with total conviction, we are suddenly aware of the nobility and splendour of the miracle of freedom, the wonder of a free will only equalled in mystery by God himself.

We can also state with conviction that each human face is destined to become an icon. We can know for certain that the haunting features of the Ethiopian child racked by hunger, faces pitifully destroyed by a hideous cancer, or those which hardly appear human, disfigured as they are by incurable defects, every face is destined to be transfigured by a light which is not of this world, which will turn them into shining icons of the living God. Even criminals whose deeds arouse our horror and disgust have God as their Father and we know that deep within them they bear a treasure, a spark of light, a spring of beauty which is destined to transform them into children of the kingdom.

In response to the tragedies which shake our world, the growing number of horrors, the injustice and hideous crimes which tear apart the human family, we can offer a clear message of ultimate hope: the faces which are disfigured by such dreadful suffering, broken by remorseless fate, innocent victims of so many kinds of violence, all are of infinite value and destined, through the vastness of God's mercy, to shine with an incomparable beauty, the beauty of the Risen Lord, icon of the Father's glory.

When we accept the Bible's teaching that human beings are made in the image of God, we discover in them a certain absolute value: we affirm their transcendence over and above the rest of creation, and in particular, we affirm that the human heart can be a source of transfiguration and sanctification, a place where God's presence can show forth at the very centre of the world. From the focal point of the human heart, the Word of God will re-create the world, communicating the divine life by the gift of the Spirit. Human beings had to be free in order that infinite freedom might find space in which to re-create the world. They needed words and faces so that the 'yes' which would unite creation to its Creator might be spoken. They had to be persons so that the glorious communion of the Trinity might be extended to the whole world. In a word, they had to be true images, and thus the fulfilment of the potential of creation.

Chapter 4
Human beings, the face of Christ

At the centre of the world is humanity; at the centre of humanity is Christ, the Word of God, creator and saviour. We discover in the face of Christ our truth as human beings, our fullest identity, that which gives us sense and purpose; it is the light of Christ's face which is destined to shine ever more clearly through our own. This human face, that of a Jewish man, is the face of God. It is the focal point of a power which will transfigure humanity and the world, and make them sacred. We are to contemplate this face, to make it ours, so that the life of the Holy Spirit may gradually be set free in us, also, as a torrent of fire. Our inconsistencies, our ugliness, all that weighs us down will be consumed in this fire. It will burn away our powerlessness which, like some worthless dross, imprisons the treasure of a never failing spring of creative liberty, continuously bestowed on us by God as he bestowed the gift of life itself.

In the glory of his crucifixion, Christ is at the world's centre, and our vocation is to be with him, there at the heart of history, where life springs forth all humanity. When we become transparent to the face of Christ within us, we too become saviours of humanity by taking our place at the foot of the cross, at the centre of the world, where the cosmic struggle between life and death is fought out. By so doing, we can achieve our highest human destiny. Insignificant in our own, wretched individuality, we can become open to the universal: we can discover a fully personal existence, that is, an existence in communion, through a sacrificial offering which opens the way to the wonderful fulfilment of divinely creative freedom, which is sanctity itself.

This is the goal for which we strive as Christians. Our aim is to take charge of the world and of history, in order to free them from despair and death and bring them to the joy of the risen Life. Following in the steps of Christ we are to join in the great task of salvation which is accomplished on Calvary, 'the place of the skull', certainly, but at the same time the place of the Resurrection. Here at the world's centre it is made possible for each one of us to let our faces become transparent to the splendour of the face of God-made-man.

Born of Mary

Jesus receives his human body from his mother whom he probably resembled closely in appearance. He is born of her into the Jewish race; through her he belongs to that extraordinary people of Israel who even today can shake the history of the world. Through her he is a child of Abraham the Semitic nomad, and heir to a complex political history marked not only by the splendid achievements of the Davidic dynasty, but also by catastrophic foreign invasions and deportations. From Mary he received the heritage of an advanced culture, whose religious intuitions, as recorded in the Bible, were destined to affect the entire world. Through his mother, Jesus is thus the heir to an extremely rich collective unconscious, which sets him at the heart of humanity and makes him fully part of it. In the human face of Jesus we can read this past, this acquired knowledge which goes back to the beginnings of the world and which he shares with each of us.

Conceived by the Holy Spirit

Faith allows us to see another dimension to this face. We read in it the fulfilment of a promise made to the ancestors of the Jewish nation and taken up in each successive generation by the prophets: the promise that God would send a saviour. The exact identity of this saviour, the extent of his mission and the way in which it would by fulfilled, were not known with any certainty until Pentecost and the outpouring of the Spirit. It is only in the light of the Spirit that Jesus' face takes on the dimension of divinity. The divine face of Jesus opens up immense depths, or rather, is open to immensity, the depths of the Word of God. Far from being enclosed in the narrow limits of features similar to our own he bears an incandescence which pierces through the darkness of our created world and opens it up to the infinity of the divine mystery.

In his face we are aware of a presence; we see in

it a love shared, a word spoken, a life offered, a wisdom which teaches, and a lordship which rules the world. But perhaps it is more truthful to say that we are aware of an absence, something utterly Beyond, an emptiness, a shadowy darkness which our eyes are powerless to penetrate. It is a face which conceals as much of the mystery as it reveals; it speaks, but remains silent; it is light, but at the same time it is surrounded by a darkness just as impenetrable as that bright cloud which indicated and concealed the presence of the unapproachable Holy of holies in the desert.

Who died and rose again

At first his face is that of a new-born baby, revealing in its incredible fragility a love which is offered in complete humility, a powerlessness which leaves itself utterly dependent on the good will of others, open to their loving adoration as well as to their murderous rage. It becomes the face of one man among many, un-remarked for thirty years. Then in his thirtieth year, love takes possession of him and transforms his whole being into a song, a flame, a cry to all humanity, telling them of the depths of God's love. He himself is revealed as the love of the Father made flesh, given to die for the world.

His face becomes that of the man of sorrows, willing to descend to the very depths of sin and misery, so as to bring to human beings the light of absolute love. Finally it is the face of the Risen Lord. The face which was disfigured by hideous suffering on the cross is transfigured by the glory of the resurrection. In this disfigured-transfigured face we can trace the wonderful story of our salvation; we see love destroyed by death only to spring up to eternity; we see the most beautiful of human beings accepting to suffer in order to rise again with a beauty which will transform the whole world.

To a unique degree, this face takes on all the anguish and horror of the human condition, transforms them into a pure offering and so makes of them the very substance of Trinitarian love.

The face of Christ, the face of humanity

His face reveals to us our own intrinsic truth. For all who are in search of themselves, in search of their identity and looking for a clue to their destiny, Christ can be held up as a mirror, a model, a 'type' (*tupos* in Greek) in which they can recognise themselves and discover the meaning which will determine the direction of their own lives. Many people today are lost and confused, a prey to all the forces which fragment society. They have come to question all values and, when shaken by misfortune, feel the injustice of undeserved suffering. Yet by looking on the face of Innocence crucified all of them can find a reason for hope and a sense of their ultimate identity as children of God. They can discover in his face that they are of supreme beauty in the eyes of the Father who calls them into his infinite fullness.

Every tear will one day be wiped away, and the terrible scars of suffering will become radiant with light, like the wounds of Christ. There are some faces indeed which are crowned with thorns, but this crown of pain will one day be transformed by God's mercy into a halo of light. The sharper the thorns and the deeper the wounds, the more radiant will be its light.

This is the message of Christianity taught by the learned, by the 'fools' of Christ's cross whom we call saints, and by all martyrs whose lives are one, long sacrificial offering. It is the mystery of the cross of Christ, the mystery of the disfigured-transfigured face which slowly becomes visible beneath our own.

The face of Christ, the face of our reconciliation

His is the face of a crucified man whose outstretched arms are a symbol of reconciliation and the gathering of all humanity into one body of which he is the head. "He is our peace; in his flesh he has made both groups into one and has broken down the dividing wall, that is, the hostility between us... that he might create in himself one new humanity... thus making peace, and might reconcile both groups to God in one body through the cross" (Eph 2:14-16). In his resurrection Christ destroyed death. No longer implying absolute finality death has become simply one step on the way to a fuller life, eternal life in union with God.

Hatred has also been overcome, not directly by the resurrection, but by the loving forgiveness which conquers evil by good. In his boundless love Christ was willing to accept the unbelievable cruelty of the passion and become an object of the hatred of the entire cosmos, revealing in the suffering of his crucified body the full extent of the powers of darkness. Yet he quenched the fury of the powerful hatred which raged against him, and by his forgiveness left it devoid of strength. He put a stop to the familiar and dangerous cycle of violence which answers hatred with ever more bitter hatred. True forgiveness destroys hatred, absorbing it in the intensity of love. Evil can thus be overcome by good and become a source of greater good.

By offering forgiveness, Christ destroyed hatred in the hearts of his executioners, in the hearts of those who had sent him to his death, and in the hearts of each one of us whose sins are a direct cause of his death. Thus "putting to death hostility" (Eph 2:16), indeed never ceasing to put it to death by his eternally present passion – "he who daily offers expiation for our violence and injustice" – Christ is able to gather into one in himself all peoples, no longer divided by barriers of hatred. "There is no longer Greek and Jew, circumcised and uncircumcised, barbarian, Scythian, slave and free; but Christ is all and in all!" (Col 3:11).

In many respects these words of St Paul read like the description of an illusive Utopia. After two thousand years of Christianity, our world is still racked by wars, racial hatred and violent nationalism which continue to erupt on all sides. Yet St Paul is in fact describing what is ours by right through the passion of Christ, and what is even now coming to be. Not only does he describe the great promise of universal reconciliation and peace for all people, he also shows us the way to achieve it, a way which is proper to Christianity.

Every great empire in the course of history has

been tempted by the idea of universality. They have all tried to impose a common order on as many nations as possible in an attempt to bring peace on earth. The familiar *Pax romana* was a reality for the countries of the Mediterranean for many centuries.

St Paul shows us a very different path to peace between nations and between individuals, one which is far more radical and far-reaching than any political approach. We are offered only one way to overcome the deep-lying hatred which tears apart our wretched humanity: the transforming power of the love which flows from the heart of Christ crucified. He is not inviting us to take part in any socio-political action or to join a revolution, but rather to allow Christ to overcome the hatred within us, to let him "offer daily expiation for our sins and our injustice" so that our human hearts may be slowly transformed, cleansed from violence and pride by the blood of the Eucharist.

Are we then to count as useless the enormous efforts made by international organisations to limit wars and introduce a minimum of justice among nations? Are the generosity and courage witnessed in countless struggles for human rights and in defence of human dignity or simply human life itself, merely in vain and doomed to inevitable failure? All these efforts are indeed indispensable and do, in fact, constitute the most important of human tasks. They are of the utmost urgency but only as far as they go.

The only truly effective solution to all these problems is to be found at the much deeper level of the human heart, the level of human freedom. All the tragedies which have marked the human condition culminate here and it is here that the change must take place. Only God is able to bring about a transformation capable of reaching to the metaphysical and spiritual roots of the human being. The reconciliation and healing of humanity must take place at such a deep level that sinful humanity inevitably proves unequal to the enormity of the task.

To "reconcile both groups to God in one body..." (Eph 2:16). This is the utopian vision of St Paul. It involves a new creation which God alone can effect. The Word of God creates us in himself and then re-creates us by his grace. It involves a new birth not according to the flesh but according to the Spirit, as Nicodemus is taught. In her mysterious role as 'mother, the Church' draws all human beings to herself and gives them new birth through the waters of Baptism, sending them out, innocent, into newness of life. Our reconciliation and unity are to be found only within the Church, the Body of Christ; she is a new creation, almost in the metaphysical sense of the term, and the power to create anew belongs to the Almighty alone.

For this reason, no political plan, no philosophy, no wisdom, no civilisation can bring into being a truly new human being. No human being can save humanity. Recent attempts in European history have ended in catastrophe, the highest and most complex ambitions inevitably resulting in the worst disasters. The idealist of the enlightenment, invented by Rousseau and the Encyclopedistes, with the lofty ideals of "liberty, equality, fraternity"; or the nineteenth century industrialist, dreaming of a bourgeois happiness made available to all by increased wealth seemingly guaranteed by the growth of industry; or more recently, a member of the superior race invented by nazism to impose a new order on the world; or again, the socialist pursuing a Marxist utopia: all have proved to be illusions and some have been the cause of genuine disasters for humankind. Humanity is infinitely greater than humanity, and God alone can be its saviour.

What we can do

Like Christ on the cross, we too can draw, or help to draw, people together. We can help to bring about the creation of a new humanity, the Body of Christ. We can destroy the hatred within ourselves, the one area for which we are truly responsible and over which we have some control, and in so doing, we can become agents of reconciliation for others in the mystery of Christian intercession which is as deep as the hiddenmost roots of love.

To intercede for others is not simply a matter of praying for them, saying a few earnest words or mumbling a few phrases on behalf of those who suffer. It is far more than this. It is to be with Christ, taking upon ourselves the suffering of the world, torn apart in our very being just as Christ is torn apart by evil and sin: it is to suffer, with Christ and in Christ, the hatred which divides our world and wounds us, body and soul, in order to transform it into an offering, into life-giving love.

Sin has deep roots in us, and violence, rather than being primarily the violence of others (who are warmongers, for example), is so much part of us that we can be considered, and indeed are, accessories to all the violence and injustice in the world. We are directly responsible for this violence; we stand in need of forgiveness and we must make atonement. We are sinners, and the only way to be cleansed is to take up our cross and follow Christ. There is no other way which can lead to innocence and no other way of bringing a little innocence into the world. Al other human beings, in so far as we are one with them, will then enter with us, through us, into the passion of Christ, to be cleansed and so restored to a life of grace in obedience to the Spirit.

The human heart is where light can conquer darkness, where innocence can take the place of the monstrous sin of the world, and where murderous hatred can be transformed into peace and solidarity. This should never be forgotten: the sin of the world is our sin; we are prisoners together, blinded by the same darkness. Our liberation is that of all people, since we share one salvation. Far from having an individual destiny, we are called to one common, universal destiny. Thus with Christ and in Christ we come to share in the work of redemption.

From one point of view, the human being is certainly a separate entity, extremely individualised, unique and unlike any other. But this person can only find fulfilment in what the philosophers call the 'reciprocity of consciousness' or in what theology might term a 'circumincession', encompassing all humanity in the image of the mystery of the Trinity. We are individuals, existing in and for ourselves, and at the same time we are destined to become 'all people', open to the universal. This is what is conveyed by our belonging to the Mystical Body of Christ which is a close solidarity both through grace and also, in a purely negative way, through sinfulness or lack of grace. We must never forget that because we can have no individual destiny, it is vital for us to work for the salvation of the whole human family, to 'expiate the sin of the world'. This is at the very heart of our vocation as Christians.

We are shown in the Bible how each individual personality finds its fulfilment only through mission, through being sent by God into the world to fulfil his promise of salvation for all. However internal our Christian life may be, it is never simply a matter of God and us, us and God. Rather God calls us to act for the redemption of the humanity. Each person finds their fulfilment in the mission or ministry entrusted to them. They find their true dimension by becoming open to the universal in a death which gives birth to eternal life for us and for others in one common hope.

The sin of the world can be tackled on the level of its disastrous political and socio-economic consequences, and this is the motivation behind all works of charity and even, in some sense, evangelisation. Or, alternatively, it can be fought at its very roots, in the deep darkness of the human heart, where the powers of evil have sway. In this radical struggle only the cross of Christ and all that it means in the way of sacrificial self-offering, can bring about victory and transform into love the hatred which consumes the human heart. This is what is meant by a life completely devoted to the passion of Christ.

In conclusion we can say that human beings, created in the image of God, hold the key to the restoration of the unity of our broken world. They are called to discover their true identity in the face of

Christ, and, by letting his face show gradually through their own, so become icons of the living God. Involved in the historical process, human beings, like Christ himself, are living through the drama of a passion which can and must lead to resurrection. Everything depends on our freedom, on the transformation of our hearts from darkness into light. Our hearts must be sanctified, cleansed and transfigured in the power of the Spirit. This is only possible through the passion and resurrection of Christ, into which we must enter so as to become 'other Christs', peace-makers, reconcilers, redeemers of each other. There is no other way in which we can help to heal the countless wounds which have torn apart the body of humanity and to restore it to its original splendour.

Chapter 5
Silence, the way of truth

For monks, the Desert is a place where living springs of the Spirit are to be found, springs of salvation, springs of redemption both for themselves and for the whole world. The living water promised to the Samaritan woman is destined to spring up to eternity in the heart of every human being, but in their passionate search for this living water the holy men and women of the Desert have chosen a particular way of life marked by celibacy, poverty, solitude, humility, obedience, fasting, vigil and prayer.

Silence plays a prominent part in these 'observances'. Its effectiveness and its importance for the spiritual life have been widely recognised by sages and spiritual teachers of various religions, and by many humanist philosophies. Certainly every Christian has a great deal to gain from seeking after silence, and this is true for any person who is in search of their own identity, their true personality, that divine spark which they sense deep within them. One need only think of Gandhi, a statesman burdened with responsibilities, who undertook to keep every Monday as a day of absolute silence, only communicating with his colleagues by written messages.

Truth in creation, truth in oneself, truth in others, truth in God: these four brief reflections will draw together some paradoxically quite wordy reflections on the rich and complex reality of silence.

The silence of creation

What is silence? It is the absence of noise, certainly; a resounding void, a kind of vacuum. But the word also suggests a suspension of time and movement, since immobility is readily associated with silence. Noise on the other hand suggests agitation. A rock in a forest, a stone placed on a table, a flower: all are there before us, with their own particular beauty, immobile, perfect in themselves. Their existence wells up into a solid, strong and beautiful presence, and with a completeness which excludes all dissonance, all noise, all disharmony. This is true silence; the peace of that which exists in the perfection of what it is meant to be.

Silence is not necessarily immobility. The vast surface of the sea, constantly rippled by waves which break on the shore in endless succession is an image of silence in the form of ceaselessly renewed life, of a living eternity. This is the silence of being, the silence of life, which is not simply the absence of sound but peace, harmony and a permanence which defies death and points to eternity.

We are living today in a world full of noise. The universe which modern humanity has fashioned for itself is dominated by noise. It is one of the main features of present day urban civilisation, and of a technical culture in which audio-visual communication has become all-pervasive. But this generalised, persistent noise is only one aspect of the considerable tension which has grown up in the relationship between human beings and the world, and of the original curse which shattered the harmony of the cosmos.

The chief obstacle which cuts off human beings from the silence of creation and the silence of others is not in fact external noise. It is the din they carry around inside themselves, the constant murmur of their unruly passions, their mad longings and their destructive impulses, which hinder them from seeing and hearing, from contemplating and receiving the world as it is.

It is all too common to come across someone walking in the forest with their radio on. They have made it impossible for themselves to see and hear the forest; they are unable to perceive the full extent of its silent beauty. Their faculties are deadened by a barrier of noise which makes them deaf and dull, incapable of any kind of communion with the beauty and truth which surround them.

More often than not we have no need of a radio to make us completely deaf to the world around us, so powerful is the internal din which assaults our minds. If we truly want to be present to each atom of life and each ray of beauty, if we want to reach the silence of creation, our hearts must be completely silent. Only silence can hear silence.

What is the silence of creation saying? Is it really silence? Is it not rather the faintest of murmurs, a subtle, unobtrusive music emanating from the depths of reality? The silence of the world speaks in words which are imperceptible but, as if by slowly penetrating our minds, it seeks to convey this message: "It is God who created me, my beauty is his. I exist only in and through the splendour of his light. The mystery of my existence, the mysterious reason for my emergence into the light, is merely the reflection of the mystery of his grace and of the immense freedom of his omnipotence."

The deeper our personal silence, the more clearly we perceive the silent murmur of creation. If our own silence is still superficial and fragile we will only make out very faintly the song that the world is singing. But if our inner space is receptive and free from interference, the song can awaken much deeper echoes in us.

Only silence of the heart allows us to reach the innermost secret of creation. Only silence enables us to hear its deepest truth, to see it as it is, not just in its aesthetic appearance or its ontological structure – aspects which appeal to the poet, the academic or the philosopher – but also in its divine dimension. The world is a symbol of God and each part of that world, from the enormity of a galaxy to the minuteness of an atom, powerfully communicates something of God to us with a richness of symbolism wonderfully echoed in the Psalms.

The silence of the heart is far more than a mere vacuum or a complete absence of thought. Instead, it is a rich and pregnant silence, the unique source of every true word spoken about the world and humanity.

Silence, the way to our truth as human beings

Who are we? What is our true face? What gives us our identity? When faced with such questions we reply by giving our profession, age, nationality, income, education etc., all of which are purely accidental, external details, of no real interest. They are facts which tell us only what can be seen, touched, and, if necessary, recorded on a machine. We are dealing here with externals, the world of appearances, things that are either trivial and insignificant, or, in the case of those who must define themselves as widows or mentally handicapped, tragic and painful.

There is however a depth of being stretching far beneath these surface appearances, whether they be bright, banal or wretched. Silence alone gives us access to the mystery of a person's inaccessible freedom. Silence alone enables us to descend to the place where our eternal identity as children of God is born. This identity has no clear definition or shape; instead it is an aspiration, a call to life and love, a call which is itself nothing other than an echo in response to the creating Word by which the utter poverty of non-existence ("You are she who does not exist", as Catherine of Siena was told) takes on a face and enters into dialogue with Love, in whom and by whom are all things.

Once all the superficial noise of passion has been quieted, silence takes us into the vast, inner space where the Word of God renews his mysterious alliance with his beloved creatures, cleansing and sanctifying them by his Spirit and drawing them to the Father, in his glory. We know from experience that the human heart can be overburdened with trivial cares, unseemly passions, vague and unhealthy longings which arise out of spiritual or earthly pride. The heart can be trapped at the purely superficial level of biological or social existence. If we want to go deeper and reach a level of existence which is truly human, where our human personality can find its divine dimension, we must go beyond the superficialities which are immediate to our consciousness. We must forget them and, if possible, efface them, in order to have access to some kind of silence and to the point at which our personality is rooted in the ultimate reality of God, creator and saviour.

Deep within us, at the very source of our personality, exists an infinite creativity and a saving power which continues to call us into existence and to recall us to itself. If we are to make out the subtle voice of this calling, the Word which, when spoken, brings us into existence – and not only us but the whole world, each created thing in its undying splendour, and each human being in the uniqueness of their personality – we must silence our hearts and minds. The sounds of finite creation, the stormy commotion of our ridiculous passions must give place to silence, in which the wonders of infinite love and peace can be set forth.

Silence then becomes another name for self-denial and renunciation. It implies the destruction of the petty, selfish ego with its paltry desires, its anger and deceitfulness, and all the passions against which the holy people of the Desert learn to struggle in order to reach that peace of which St Benedict speaks (*hesychia* in Greek), and of which the Lord says: "Peace I leave with you; my peace I give to you. I do not give to you as the world gives" (Jn 14:27).

There are in fact two ways of finding peace. The first is to be in a position to benefit from all the good things of life: security, comfort and various pleasures. When we are happy, relaxed, satisfied and free of suffering, we are at peace. Such is the peace which the world gives, but how very fragile it is! The peace of Christ is the only true peace, and it takes a very different form. It belongs to those who no longer demand anything for themselves, who have renounced everything, who surrender themselves completely and willingly to all that happens and who live in a joyful, peaceful and loving acceptance of all that the Father wills in his wisdom. This peace comes from the renunciation of every private and selfish desire and from an intimate relationship with the infinite wisdom and goodness which govern the immensity of the world down to its smallest detail.

Silence is like a privileged path leading towards an inwardness in which our truth as human beings is spoken and lived. Here our eternal identity gradually takes shape, and our true personality is traced in outline, although it cannot fully emerge until our false, artificial and compulsive persona have disappeared, persona which are continually created by our imagination and our complexes, our anxieties and our day dreams.

Who, then, is this true, inner self who is found in silence and who gradually emerges from our depths in the light of the Spirit? The gospels readily give it the features of a child. St John speaks of being 'born from above', of becoming once again like little children. St Peter talks of the utter weakness and innocence of new-born babies, so implying a need for total dependence on the Father. The baby, newly born from on high, can say only one word: 'Abba, Father!' This is the word which the Spirit murmurs within us, and we can only hear it if there is silence in our hearts. Our deepest being finds expression in the Spirit until it becomes, in the manner of Jesus, nothing other than a longing which reaches out to the Father and a complete surrender to his wisdom.

All Christians are called to share this experience, and all do to varying degrees, depending on the level of transparency and silence they have reached through divine grace. But, we may ask, how far does this union with the Word of God go? Does it lead to a complete identification, as St Paul's words suggest: "...it is no longer I who live, but it is Christ who lives in me"? Is the self absorbed into God, so losing its separate identity as in the experience of 'Advaita" sought by Hindus? When all other things are left behind, silence opens up a way to the very foundation of our being, and to an absolute interiority; but is this truly God or something other than God? All the great mystics have raised this question: "I in You, You in me, my 'self' lost in You so that You alone remain."

In other words: does mystical union take the form of a marriage, consistent with a dialogue between a You and a me; or is it rather the discovery of God as the ultimate dimension of every person, the ultimate depths of their being, in which case he could only be expressed by silence? Theology provides a very definite response to this question: human beings always retain their freedom before God and thus their relationship with him takes the form of a dialogue. However, certain contemplatives have described a slightly different kind of experience, in which apophatic silence is seen as the highest form of union with God. Such a silence involves a real loss of self; the 'I' which is capable of speech and thought is absorbed in a totally unknowable Absolute. We find this tendency in the writings of Evagrius of Pontus, Denys the Areopagite, and Meister Eckhart, the *Cloud of Unknowing* and certain passages in St John of the Cross.

These are all academic questions of real but not vital interest. "...You have hidden these things from the wise and the intelligent and have revealed them to infants" (Mt 11:25). The Lord sets us back on the right path: are little children aware of whether they are speaking or silent? Is there really such a radical difference between speech and silence? Is not every silence, provided that it is true silence, pregnant with a word which aims to convey that which is beyond words. Could not silence be just another name for the burning desire which brings forth words only to consume them as its ardour increases?

Silence as a way into the truth in others

If we are to listen to another person, we must first be silent. We must be willing to create an empty space within ourselves in which the words spoken by that other person can fully resonate, and where their intimate song can ascend. If we have not made silence within ourselves, their inner song will remain inaudible. The secret melody of their suffering or their joy, their anxiety or their hope, in which they seek to express their own depths, the best or the most painful reality about themselves, will remain incomprehensible and totally foreign to us, even if the sound of their words reaches our ears.

In order to become truly capable of listening to someone else, we must silence our preoccupations, our prejudices, our fears of being found out, our longing to dominate or seduce. Only then can we hear and see that other person in all the complexity of their personality. Above all, we will be capable of something far more important than any simple psychological intuition; we will be able to share in the mystery of the divine Word which makes them people with creative freedom, persons in the fullest sense of the term, inviolable and absolute.

A silent heart is essential if we are to sense within another person the image of God, the face of Christ which is slowly trying to emerge from beneath the accumulated debris of sin, the sometimes dramatic distortions imposed by heredity or the negative or tragic circumstances of life. Our hearts must be pure like clear mirrors – not simply neutral, but loving – which can reflect the future beauty of that other person, a beauty as yet still hidden. A silent heart is a living mirror which calls forth life. It gives back to others not simply a reflection of their present appearance but also an image of the transfigured face which they are destined to wear in the future; this is the glorious face, full of goodness and peace, which they already carry within them from Baptism.

Every person has a face imposed by sin, an easily seen, outer face often distressing for themselves and for others. But they also have a face of light, an inner, hidden face, shaped in secret by the grace of God and which will one day, in the light of the Holy Spirit, become an icon shining with divine holiness.

This icon is the face which is already present in us but still hidden. We can help to make it appear by calling it forth with a loving word spoken from our deepest self, the self which is truly silent, humble and welcoming. In contrast, the superficial self which is besieged by noise, the 'hateful' self which Pascal describes as so selfish and proud, knows only how to criticise and reject, and is capable only of destruction. Only a word spoken from the depths of our inner silence can be truly life-giving; this word alone can reveal to others their true depths, their identity, hidden in the silence of eternity, and bring forth the new being which yearns to be born within them.

To be authentic, dialogue must be a communion between two silences. Most encounters take the form of a noisy confrontation between two chattering outward selves which more often than not remain completely deaf to each other. Here we find a paradox: the silence which results from interiority, far from being the sign of an egoistic withdrawal into oneself, can be seen as the one, necessary condition for genuine openness to communion with others.

Silence, the way to God

Silence is just one of the ascetical disciplines which together make up the monastic life. As far as it is possible for them, all people, whether or not they are monks in the desert, certainly have something to gain from silence, in the way of a discovery of peace and unity within themselves. If we are to be recharged with spiritual and physical strength, we need to withdraw our senses, even if only temporarily, from the excessive stimulation fired at them by the modern world. Once unity, peace and harmony have been restored, our senses can be more easily directed towards the one thing necessary, to which we give the name God.

There are two sides to silence as an ascetical practice. Firstly there is the purely material aspect: it involves a rejection of all noise, an elimination of sound which can be achieved in isolation, whether behind closed doors or out in the open. This silence gives our life a permanent or temporary structure, which is the norm in monastic life. Invaluable because of its rarity in our world today, this kind of silence is, nevertheless, something completely external, a quantity which can be mechanically evaluated in terms of decibels.

Of far greater spiritual value is the silence which takes the form of a limitation or rejection of verbal communication. This kind of silence involves talking as little as possible, or not at all. Because voluntary limitation demands an almost constant effort on the part of the individual, it has a far greater spiritual significance and potential than any purely objective reduction in the number of decibels reaching our ears.

We must bear in mind that these two kinds of outer silence are relative. In any place, however hidden away and isolated, there will always be a minimum of noise, and verbal communication cannot be withheld indefinitely. Its relative nature suggests that objective silence is no more than a means, a circumstance of life or a straightforward exercise, a discipline which should never be offered as an absolute. Holiness does not necessarily depend on silence!

What is the significance of this discipline for the spiritual life? Outer silence is obviously an aid to inner silence. Along with other ascetical practices its aim is to enable the soul to be silent before God, to attain to that peace and purity of heart which will allow it to receive God's gift of the Spirit, and to live in intimate union with the Lord. When we voluntarily reduce or refrain from verbal exchanges with others, we put an end to one major source of the petty, external distractions over which we waste such vast amounts of our intellectual and spiritual energies. We all know by experience how enervating chatter can be; it wears down our personality and submerges us in trivialities. It distracts us, in the sense that it leads us away from our true selves and reduces our inner unity to a sterile inconstancy.

We are not however denying the fact that human speech is not only good but actually one of the greatest of human privileges. It is the image within each human being of the eternal Word uttered by the Father. Speech is self-expression, the gift of oneself to and in another. Speech brings about a spiritual communion of love, creating in every truly deep encounter a living parable of the mystery of the Trinity. Speech is truth and sustains truth; words of truth communicate life and love and in return bring about spiritual union. Human speech can however be stripped of this wonderful reality and degraded until it is nothing more than the sound of chattering voices. Lies and bitter criticism can pervert it into an instrument of deceit or even destruction, capable not only of ruining a person's reputation but also of dealing a fatal wound to their very being.

St Benedict and the holy people of the Desert recommend silence not for any exalted reasons but simply in a modest and realistic attempt to avoid the many ways in which human speech can be corrupted. Speech remains fundamentally good; it is simply a question of preventing its abuse. This involves a measure of discipline which in fact goes much further than appears. When we look for the reasons behind useless or evil words we see that they arise from the thoughts which trouble the heart of the monk or the Christian. If the heart has not been cleansed and has not achieved a state of peace, *hesychia*, complete transparency to the divine light, its thoughts will be futile or perverse, and will overflow in words which are equally futile and perverse. "For out of the abundance of the heart the mouth speaks" (Mt 12:34).

This brings us back to the ultimate question: how do we achieve this silence of the heart? Here we find ourselves at the very core of our ideal of the Christian life, whether monastic or not. It is an ideal which certainly cannot be defined solely in terms of contemplation, of a knowledge of God sought and granted essentially in prayer. Instead it must have a wider definition as an ideal of transformation and purification for the human heart, allowing it to become united to God, transformed by him and made holy by his Holy Spirit. When we speak of conversion, purification or sanctification, or use words richer in theological content such as transfiguration in the Spirit, or 'deification', we are attempting to express the mystery of the complete encounter between God and humanity, which is the basis of the good news proclaimed in the Gospel.

The phrase 'silence of the heart', or *hesychia*, attempts to convey a reality of the same order. It implies a union with God, since silence and peace are not simply the absence of noises and distractions but are indwelt by a Presence which finds its expression in fullness and abundance of life. This silence is not empty and soundless; it is a pregnant silence, the silence of a communion in which words fail, rendered insignificant before a reality so complete and full.

There are several images which convey an idea of what is involved: the silence in a mother's eyes as she leans over her child, the silence in the faces of two people united in an embrace, the silence which emanates from something of 'absolute' beauty, such as a painting, a landscape, or a piece of music which robs one of words. But we must not be mistaken about this silence: there is no spectacular ecstasy, no absorption, no trance-like state which suspends thought and interrupts normal life. It is an otherworldly silence, found at depths which defy nature but do not deny its freedom. And it is something far more than this: deep silence frees the personality, bestows on it a kind of sovereign ease, a royal peace. When someone finds the living springs of silence and attains to deep peace, it shows in the radiance of their bearing; they are new people, freed from their fears and complexes and from their pride. They appear truly free because they have been freed from themselves. In the beyond within themselves they have found the springs of divine peace, of true life and eternal silence.

Rather than being the silence of divine peace, the silence of the soul is far more often the silence of patience, humility and good nature deliberately maintained in the most difficult of circumstances. It is the silence of Job, a man who was ruined, sick, jeered at, but who said "I lay my hand on my mouth" (Job 40:4); a man who bowed to a wisdom too great for his understanding, a wisdom which shattered the narrow limits of a world of short-sighted happiness and justice and crushed him in its ruins.

It is also the silence of vigil, the silence of a love which keeps awake, overcoming the heaviness of sleep and the dullness of despair, in the knowledge that the Bridegroom will come at last, far on in the night.

It is the silence of dawn, when the shadows fade and the surge of new life sets the heart pounding with fresh hope. The Lord is coming; he is knocking at the door, asking to be let in. The world becomes transparent, present to an eternity which floods it with light through the thin veil of longed-for death, and transforms it into its own likeness so that all distinctions between this world and the next disappear.

It is also the silence of noon, the hour of the annunciation, when Presence becomes fire, intimacy becomes boundless and interiority opens into infinity; the hour of completion, when the cosmos reveals its marvellous truths and the purely external is turned into interiority within the human spirit.

It is the silence of evening, when peace shrouds

all things in perfect offering, when the fullness of that which is, completes its journey back to the silent spring in which all speech is rendered useless.

There is also a silence of consummation in which the living flame glows with warmth, yet painfully burns away all that does not belong to it; and a silence of distress in which the Beyond becomes even more distant and our finite selves know their own powerlessness in the face of the infinity which confronts them.

Finally, there is the silence of Love in which the Beloved is everything; an unknowable gulf, an immeasurable splendour beyond all joy, all tenderness, all wonder, beyond what words can say...

Chapter 6
Solitude – desolation and blessing

Is not happiness closely connected with the joy of togetherness? Do not friendship and solidarity rank before riches and power as giving the greatest pleasure? Is not the relationship between a man and a woman, when lived out in tenderness and mutual understanding, the most attractive form of human happiness imaginable? Is not perfect happiness, the paradise so ardently sought by all forms of religious desire, a union with God and in God, a total communion with all the beauty and goodness of creation?

Set against the brightness of this ideal, solitude, isolation and severed communion seem to be perfect images of unhappiness, and to indicate a deliberate choosing of suffering and death. Solitude is indeed more often than not a very negative experience. Solitude is frightening. The different forms it can take – desertion, exclusion, or deprivation – are synonymous with death.

Why, then, do some people voluntarily choose a life of solitude? What makes them flee from others and go into the Desert to confront the emptiness of solitude? How is the desolation which accompanies solitude turned, for them, into blessing and abundance of life? Is there some kind of miraculous formula there which can transform poverty into riches, despair into rejoicing, and death into springs of life?

A fundamental human experience

We have an urgent need of other people. Their friendship, the services they provide and all the various forms of interaction which are taking place continuously, are vital for our survival. Our dependence on others goes deeper than a plant's dependence on its roots, or a cell's dependence on the organism which surrounds it. Thus any separation from others, any withdrawal from the solidarity of life which supports us, exposes us to the risk of death. This is why solitude can so easily result in distress. Someone who is lonely and 'deserted', forgotten and rejected by others is a prey to anguish. There is the anguish of a child alone in the dark, the anguish of an elderly person who is totally isolated; of the orphan deprived of its parents; of the unemployed person, excluded from the world of work; of the drug addict and the delinquent, rejected by society, pushed out into an underworld of scorn, suspicion and guilt. Any deviation, any failure or inability to conform to the social model excludes people, leaving them isolated from the group through a breakdown in the dialogue of human solidarity.

Most people tend to see solitude as desolation. Human beings are not meant to be alone and they know it in their heart of hearts. Much of the research carried out on the human personality reveals that dialogue between an 'I' and a 'you' is extremely important in structuring the personality and allowing it to establish its own existence. It is a metaphysical necessity: the 'I' can only affirm its subjectivity in relation to a 'you', and if the latter withdraws from it, or is lacking, the 'I' is weakened and overwhelmed by the anguish of not being recognised by others.

A vital anguish

This is what makes solitude so hard to bear and so frightening. It destroys, or at least threatens a person's unity. In solitude people are confronted with their own weakness and their sheer inability to be self-sufficient. They discover that they are finite, limited creatures, dependent on others and on the world around them for their very survival. Flight from solitude seems to be a legitimate and necessary reflex. Is it not commonly said that nature abhors a vacuum?

The destruction of human relationships is often accompanied by a loss of material security; people are deprived of their familiar surroundings, the objects which keep them company and which are necessary to their existence – an existence so fragile that it must be securely protected. This impoverishment results in a kind of emotional isolation which is made all the more hard to bear in that it makes us aware of the emptiness inside us. The most important aspect of solitude, in terms of its significance for the spiritual life, is the discovery that at the core of our being there is complete emptiness, a space containing nothing. This is the space where we suffer and weep, where we are desperately alone, prey to a terrifying, incurable sickness of heart, since the gulf we have discovered is devoid of meaning and makes a mockery of all our reasons for living. All our most basic certainties appear groundless, providing no answers to the boundless question which arises from the emptiness we have suddenly come across in the depths of our being.

We are totally unaware of this gulf and of the sickness of heart it causes, as long as we remain untouched by the experience of desolation which reveals it. Desolation brings to light the unclosable chasm which opens into the nothingness within every being who is subject to contingency and relativity. The chasm remains unnoticed as long as it is concealed beneath a mass of possessions and the superficialities of a world of external appearances. But there comes a time when total deprivation, true solitude and genuine distress result in a first-hand experience of the terrifying absurdity we find so often described. Human beings are not whole and entire, and the discovery that they are finite opens up a wound which cannot be healed.

Solitude and maturity

This experience of solitude is not wholly negative; it is a necessary step on the road to maturity. When a baby is thrust from its mother's womb at birth and the umbilical cord is cut, it begins an independent existence, an existence destined to become increasingly individualised and autonomous. Violent severance from the surroundings of its mother's womb is doubtless a traumatic experience; but by means of this separation, the baby is plunged into a solitude which marks the beginning of the road towards the blossoming of its personality, until it reaches adulthood and becomes a fully human person. Once distanced from the mother's womb and thrown into solitude, the child is set free from the smothering closeness of symbiosis and can begin to emerge as a subject in relation to its mother. So begins a first dialogue which will enable it to develop in freedom the capacity to accept or reject, to love or to hate. For the child, the trauma of birth is a first experience of solitude and autonomy, opening up the journey towards personality.

This need for differentiation is given particular emphasis in psychoanalysis. There must be a break away from immediate surroundings, from parents and social background, if the personality is to reach maturity and achieve a higher level of dialogue with others. The personality can fully emerge only when it has broken away from the anonymity of the social group. Among individuals, the possibility of dialogue implies a certain distance between people which allows them to recognise their mutual otherness. Although traumatic and negative for the victims themselves, the various experiences of rejection and solitude can become opportunities for new birth; they can lead to the severing of ties which results in a new maturity and to a fuller, richer relationship with the social group. When a militant member is expelled from the Party; when someone is excommunicated from their church; when a partner is rejected or a neglected child runs away; when a delinquent is excluded from society; when anyone is cast out, forced into unwanted solitude and condemned to loneliness, they are suddenly confronted with the fact of their liberty. They are presented with an opportunity to re-affirm their identity, to initiate a new and richer dialogue with the group from which they have been 'born' by violent rejection, an expulsion which can be seen in terms of delivery. But not all situations result in successful birth; there may be painful miscarriages which leave people deeply wounded in their humanity, bruised and broken, cut off for life from a whole area of their being: solitude can so often destroy the personality.

Solitude and evil spirits

Sociological solitude which is imposed rather than freely chosen soon proves to be a kind of hell; a place in which all the spirits of evil are unleashed. When unemployed people are denied the chance of a useful occupation and scornfully pushed aside, they often give in to the demon of despair. Some may even go as far as suicide. Delinquents and outcasts of all kinds are a prey to an often implacable hatred of the society which has excluded them. They are taken over by the terrifying demons of bitterness, scorn, violent despair, and the nihilism which Dostoevsky described at length in his famous novel *The Devils*, which prepared the way for the revolution of Russian society. All human beings who have experienced a breakdown of communion, all who have been excluded, all who are condemned to solitude are at risk from a dangerous inner fragmentation and threatened with disintegration by the demons which rage within them.

It is surprising to note that these demons generally stay hidden, or at least their presence remains fairly well concealed, as long as the equilibrium ensured by successful social integration is maintained. As long as individuals are happy and surrounded by the protective cocoon of respect and friendship, as if by their mother's womb, they can be almost completely oblivious to the demons they carry inside. But once difficulties arise and they find themselves excluded and rejected, the demons are unleashed. A person then experiences the hell of solitude. Shaken to their foundations, they face the anguish and despair which result in a disintegration of their personality. This is why many of those who live on the fringes of our society only manage to escape this inner crisis by suicide or by the slow death of drug addiction.

Although we may not have gone quite this far, which one of us has not experienced the bitterness and anger of being unloved, misunderstood, excluded or pushed to the edges of the social or family circle? What demons have we not felt stirring in the depths of our hearts, sometimes causing such strange inner turmoil?

Monastic solitude

Those who live in the city, exhausted by the noise and confusion of urban life, may well be attracted by the silence and peace of solitude in nature. In the same way, the religious who is weary of the irksome demands of the common life may dream of solitude: nature is so beautiful, it would be so good to be able to live in peace by oneself... St Jerome himself was attracted by this mirage and has left us a pleasantly idyllic description of life in the Desert. But we find a very different attitude among the ancient monks who, curiously enough, claimed to go into the Desert not in search of peace, but for combat; not for life with God and his angels, as one might expect, but for a confrontation with demons. This myth of battle with the evil spirits which are supposed to live in the desert – a myth which has clear roots in biblical as well as secular culture – communicates a deep spiritual experience. St Anthony, the father of monasticism, is famous for the temptations he suffered at the hands of the devil, while he was living shut up in a tomb. We are all aware of how iconographers have revelled in these temptations, and how they have haunted the imaginations of generations of Christians and monks. The demons were pictured as horrifying monsters, bent on terrorising the unfortunate ascetic and sometimes physically ill-treating him.

Anyone who is living in the Desert is, in fact, at risk; the very extremity of their life-style quickly reduces them to extremes. Not only are they having to cope with separation from other human beings, they are also experiencing the dreadful nights described by St John of the Cross, in which God himself seems distant, absent from a life which yet longs to depend entirely on him. This experience of extreme desolation, of utter rejection, of void, cannot but shake the very foundations of a personality which has been uprooted, unbalanced and subjected to the meaninglessness of incomprehensible suffering. In a chaos which destroys all points of reference and all sense of direction, the personality is left sense-less, only a brief step away from madness.

A young, Coptic peasant of the 3rd century, Antony was played upon by the terrifying superstitions of a still prevalent paganism; he was living under the pressures of a rigorous ascetic discipline, shut away in the austerity of a sinister tomb, and, in addition, tested by the 'night of the spirit': it is hardly surprising that he experienced a kind of disintegration of the personality, along with delirium and hallucinations. Passing beyond the bounds of rationality, the elemental impulses of the psyche inevitably emerged in the form of terrifying and demonical hallucinations, bringing in their wake the disturbing phantoms of the pagan collective unconscious and the phantoms which are bound up with the individual whose life history they symbolically reflect.

It is at such moments of testing, whether or not they are accompanied by phantoms, that demons appear and great rifts are brought to light in the personality which has been shaken to its very foundations. These rifts prove to be haunts where terrible demons lie in ambush; the demons of bitterness, wounded pride, suicidal despair, blasphemy and doubts about the existence of a God who is all too absent. These times of inner turmoil, such as occur in every human existence at moments of great disruption or trauma, can be the pangs of new birth; the darkness of night which heralds the dawn.

Not everyone is called to face the particular trials of St Antony, but each one of us has, sooner or later, to confront the terrible demons which we carry inside: the demons of aggression, resentment, pride, sadness, despair... It is at times like this that the deep wisdom of the Desert proves its true capacity; in our distress, it shows us a way to salvation. The ancient monks were, in fact, skilled explorers of the inner hell which each one of us carries inside, and they laboured to bring to it the peace of Christ, *hesychia*, won by a long, hard struggle against 'evil thoughts'.

In his rule, St Benedict urges us to shatter these evil thoughts against Christ. The force of the word 'shatter', indicates that this is no easy task: such thoughts can be extremely violent, powerful enough to lead to a disintegration of the personality; but they are so deep-rooted that a great deal of time is needed before the grace, strength and peace radiant in the face of Christ are able to make an end of them.

The struggle against these thoughts is a vast and complex undertaking: in order to assuage resentment, banish anxiety, heal inferiority or superiority complexes, overcome depression, control aggression, integrate sexuality, correct delusions of grandeur or counteract the hysterical outbursts of frustrated emotions etc., we must call on all the resources available to traditional Christian asceticism, psychotherapy or even psychoanalysis. It is a particularly exacting task to attempt to heal the wounds of the past and cleanse the memory, as St John of the Cross puts it, or to undergo the 'healing of memories', to quote a modern author, and so bring light into the most painful, most wounded and most defective corners of our unconscious – this strange world so brilliantly explored since Freud. It is a task which results not only in a certain degree of natural balance but, from the Christian and monastic point of view, in nothing less than holiness or peace of heart.

The holy people of the Desert lay great emphasis on the fact that 'evil thoughts' can only be eliminated with the help of Christ. Moral philosophy and psychotherapy are quite unable to heal the depths of the human soul. They are unable to dry up the poisonous springs of bitterness, of pride etc.; what is required is the grace of Christ, the transfiguring radiance of the Holy Spirit's saving power. Only Christ can heal our wounds, and if he is to do this, we must first offer them to him, exposing them to the power of his redeeming love.

When terrible thoughts assail us, when hatred, dislike of others, doubt or sadness take hold of us, we are able, in faith, to call on Christ. We can tell him again and again of our suffering, descend with him into the depths of our hearts, wounded, bewildered and racked with anxiety or rage as they are, and then, like the centurion, the Phoenician woman, the man born blind and so many others, we can say to him: Lord, you can do all things...

The path towards the obscurity of our inner selves, towards the terrible hell which each one of us carries within, often without our knowing, must be travelled over and over again; but it is to be travelled in the company of Christ until he brings us healing. Only then will the old humanity, ill-tempered and selfish, proud and anxious, paralysed by all sorts of complexes, gradually make room for the child of the kingdom, re-born from above by the waters of the Spirit. This is what it means truly to live out the Gospel and to know its saving power. But we must still distance ourselves from these thoughts so that we can see them as the evils they are. To begin with we identify ourselves completely with our anger, our bitterness and our perverted impulses, and, more often than not, we fully comply with these passions and consider it perfectly legitimate to give way to them. Students who are in despair after a failure, unemployed people made bitter by rejection, a divorced man full of resentment against his former wife, would all consider that they have a right to feel as they do. They need to undergo a real conversion in order to turn to Christ and ask for the healing which is so often just another name for humility, pardon, acceptance and sacrificial offering.

While a child's tantrum can be calmed fairly quickly, the same cannot be said for the impulses which emanate from the very depths of the unconscious. These are deep wounds, frustrations and emotional traumas which date back to early childhood or even to the time before birth; they emerge as chronic or recurrent depression, outbursts of hysteria and a whole range of mental disorders. There is no limit to the number of ways in which distress can be manifested, but the infinite mercy and boundless compassion of God-made-man, he who was willing to become the 'man of sorrows', a man who knew all our sorrows, offers us a way to overcome each one of them; a Passover which leads to resurrection and a higher, more abundant life. We must affirm with all the strength of our faith, based as it is on the witness of all the saints, that the grace of Christ and the anointing of the Holy Spirit can, like a soothing balm, not necessarily heal these wounds completely, but change them into stigmata, radiant with a transfiguring glory which flows from the fullness of the crucified man, God-made-man.

When the wounds which we bear, however serious, cease to be merely a painful consequence of fatality and of the injustices imposed at random by heredity, history and all that has burdened humanity since the Fall, they become, or can become, positive signs of a freely made offering, a willing sacrifice presented in love and thus a possible source of the perfect joy referred to by Francis of Assisi. From this moment on, the spring of 'evil thoughts' gradually runs dry and grace begins to work in us in the place of despair and rage. The road is usually long, though God in his grace may shorten it for some; everything depends, in fact, on our openness to the light of mercy which penetrates to the depths of the soul, sometimes at the cost of a real inner upheaval which lays bare the very foundations of our being.

Solitude as blessing

If death is to open up into life and desolation be turned into blessing, we must be prepared to face extremes. Solitude places us at the world's end which finally proves to be death itself. The Gospel tells us again and again: if there is no death, there can be no newness of life. We must take up our cross and follow Christ on the long, long road to Calvary. In the depths of desolation we can become children of God; here it is that our status as children is gradually shaped through the continual, intense, heart-rending cry which, in and with Christ, we utter without ceasing: 'Abba, Father!' and again, 'My God, my God, why have you forsaken me?' (Mt 27:46).

While we remain within the confines of this world, hemmed in by our trivial, wretched ambitions, we cannot become children of God. The universe we have built for ourselves in our pride must be torn apart by desolation so that, moved by the Spirit, we cry out the Father's name; a cry for help, a cry of trust which identifies us with Christ, whose sonship was offered in its entirety as a willing sacrifice, a eucharistic song.

The Holy Spirit teaches us to celebrate this Eucharist in the midst of the desolation of our solitude, but such a celebration is only made possible when death itself has become an act of grace; only then can it take on its full reality and depth. "Happy are those whom you discipline, O Lord" (Ps 94:12). Rebellion against unmerited suffering, unbearable frustration, the injustice of being handicapped, despair at being rejected or at losing a loved one; all of these can be the starting point of the work of grace. There is nothing easy and childish about it; it is eucharistic grace, just as the passion and death of our Saviour are called blessed in the liturgy.

How can there be joy in the midst of our sorrow? Is there some kind of masochism involved? Or is it perhaps, as human wisdom would have it, due to a sense of the hereafter, an intuition that fulfilment can be achieved through the destruction of the limited, fragile happiness which is keeping us from a higher form of joy? According to this way of thinking, the world is nothing and God is everything; so why not let the world perish and God be all? But we cannot go along with this.

Christianity teaches us something quite different. In conclusion to a long passage of teaching on perfect joy, Francis of Assisi dictated these fervent words to Brother Leo: "If we endure hardship patiently and cheerfully, thinking of the sufferings of the blessed Christ and knowing that we must endure all things in love, O Brother Leo, write down that that would be perfect joy" (*Fioretti* no. 8). The pain of desolation can only be transformed into perfect joy through union with the Word of God; it is a way to fullness of life only because through it, the Word of God, who is the happiness of all the saints, involves us in his own adventure of death and resurrection. The Word of God becomes our all through this experience of death, in which we are buried in him as in the waters of Baptism. In the extremity of desolation the way is opened up for us to become one with the crucified Word; this is the moment of perfect joy, of an ecstasy which leads to forgetfulness of self, sacrificial offering, and the highest degree of life-giving love. Those who know, know; those who do not, do not. Let us give thanks to the Father who has "hidden these things from the wise and the intelligent and revealed them to infants" (Lk 10:21) and to all *poverellos* everywhere, the little, poor ones whom we are destined to become one day, when the great desolation of solitude has created in us a space for resurrection, a space from which will spring the eucharistic blessing of victory over death.

If we accept its challenge, the Desert reveals to us

the existence of that inner desert which we all carry within us. We find it to be the haunt of terrible demons – for as long, that is, as the light of Christ, his peace, his mercy and the blessings of his power have not assured, at the price of a long, hard struggle, the triumph of life in the silent enjoyment of his ineffable presence.

Chapter 7
The Eucharist, sacrament of our solitude

There is a physical desert, inhabited by a few exceptional men and women who are called to live there; but more importantly, there is an inner Desert, into which each one of us must one day venture. It is a void; an empty space for solitude and testing. Although we might suppose this Desert to be situated at the farthest bounds of the earth, it is, in fact, to be found at the very centre. It is from this precise point that the world and humanity can become a Eucharist, a burning bush, alight with the power of the Spirit.

The Eucharist is, in fact, at the centre of human history and of the history of God's dealings with humanity. It is the alpha and omega, incorporating within it all of time and the whole world of material reality. But for each of us, too, it is a burning glass, opening a way into our innermost depths. Through the Eucharist, we can approach the very centre of our being, which is at the same time the centre of the world.

Let us go back to the words of Jesus: "I am the living bread that came down from heaven. Whoever eats of this bread will live forever" (Jn 6:51).

The Eucharist as bread

In the Eucharist we use bread which is made from flour. Thousands of grains of wheat are ground to make the flour which is then kneaded with water and salt and baked in the oven once the yeast has made it rise. This bread is indeed the 'work of human hands', and also the fruit of the earth and of the universe as a whole. Sun and rain are essential if the wheat is to grow and ripen. The wheat itself is the product of a long evolutionary process which began, at the very origins of the world, with the first subatomic particles which formed the dust out of which the whole multitude of galaxies emerged.

The history of the world from its first beginnings is encapsulated in this piece of bread which, in addition, clearly shows the marks of human intelligence and the human ability to transform. In this bread, matter is somehow powerfully imbued with spirit, worked on and transformed, made spiritual by the activity of human intelligence.

But bread is also food. Once eaten, digested and absorbed, it will become our body. The different ingredients from which it is composed will go to make up the most minute fibres of our bones, muscles and nervous system. It will become our very being through assimilation, a fusion more intimate than we can possibly imagine.

The Eucharist as living bread

The living bread which came down from heaven brings with it the very life of God. In the gift of his Word, God himself comes to us in light, creativity, love and holiness. The Word of God gives himself to us as food, thus effecting the highest possible form of union in love. In the Eucharist, God's substance becomes ours; we are made divine. 'God was made human', and then bread and wine, 'so that human beings might be made God'.

This is a summary of the whole of God's great plan for humanity: a plan to draw human beings to himself, to absorb them into himself so that they might become one with him in perfect love, in a relationship of such transparency that no husband and wife could imagine anything more perfect. God loves human beings as no lover has ever loved. The fervent poetry of the Song of Songs is an attempt to convey something of the ardour of this love, but its success is limited.

"God so loved the world that he gave his only Son" (Jn 3:16). This is the culmination of God's love; here his purpose for humanity and for the whole of creation is fulfilled. But the gift of his son is not limited to the incarnation in the womb of the Virgin Mary and the subsequent passion and resurrection of Jesus of Nazareth. All of humanity is to receive the Word of God and enter into the pain and glory of the passion and resurrection. The Eucharist is the unique means by which the mystery of the Word of God-made-man reaches all humanity, to incorporate it in the wonderful plan according to which he came down to earth from heaven, to die and to rise again in his glorious ascension to the Father. The Eucharist, in fact, allows us to share in the death and resurrection of the Son of God; we are drawn after him, to enter ever more deeply into the life of his divinity each time the Eucharist is celebrated anew anywhere in the world.

The Eucharist as symbol and language

In order to communicate our ideas and feelings we use words, gestures and various kinds of body language. Speaking and writing are physical gestures by which we seek to convey an idea or a feeling, and in the same way, a hand-shake, a hug or a lovers' embrace attempt to express the meeting of hearts by means of bodily contact. Contact and communication can never take place between minds and hearts; the body must always act as go-between, and thus a certain degree of outwardness is always inevitable. The body is at one and the same time both a means to perfect communication and an obstacle to it. Bodies can be separated by distance – 'Out of sight, out of mind' as the saying goes; the heart turns away when the body is absent. This is why perfect lovers like Tristan and Isolde seek the fullest realisation of their love in death, which does away with the body.

In the Eucharist the body of Christ – through which the Apostles were able to encounter the Word of God: "...what we have looked at and touched with our hands, concerning the word of life..." (1 Jn 1:1) – becomes our food. In that moment it disappears completely, it is assimilated and becomes the very substance of the one who receives it. This body which has been given as food ceases to be an obstacle and becomes instead the perfect means of spiritual union and the communication of minds. The Eucharist can thus be seen as the most perfect, most transparent language of love, the ideal symbol of the intimate union of the Spirit of Christ with our own spirit. The Holy Spirit which is one with the Word of God is given to us so that we might become one, new being in Christ, with him and through him. Here too love and death are closely linked, but not as they were for Tristan and Isolde! Christ's body had to suffer death on the cross so that from his pierced heart might flow forth blood and water, symbols of the Spirit of love given to the world and which the Eucharist aims to spread abroad through all of time and space. The Eucharist is indeed the language of the highest and most far-reaching love.

The Eucharist as sacrifice

The Eucharist is a sacrament of sacrifice: Christ's sacrifice and our own. 'Sacrifice' is an unpleasant word; it immediately suggests something painful, something purely negative, a deprivation with no promise of compensation. Making a sacrifice means depriving ourselves of something to which we are attached or which we enjoy and, in the context of the major religions, it can involve the slaughter of an animal or of a prisoner of war. In fact, in its original and fullest sense, the word is used to refer to what has been made sacred (*sacrum facere*) or which has been consecrated by an offering to God. Every moment of our lives, every human gesture, every feeling of joy and happiness, every beautiful thing we see can become a sacrifice, a gift freely offered to God, not by destruction or renunciation but by acceptance in the light of grace. Each morning we can offer our day to the Lord, we can make it a 'sacrifice' of joy and thankfulness, and of hope, too, for his goodness toward us: a sacrifice opens up dialogue and calls for reciprocity. Our whole lives are to become sacrifice, gift and offering.

So why is sacrifice associated with pain, hardship, privation and death? Firstly, it seems, because or our overriding instinct to close in on ourselves and our deep-seated reluctance to open up to other people. It is this negation of generosity which we call sin. Sin shapes us at our very depths as separate entities, shut in on ourselves, stuck in relationships of juxtaposition and opposition and incapable of communion. Because it involves a threat to our security and tranquillity, or the loss or destruction of what belongs to us, the act of giving or the lowering of our defences is inevitably experienced as something costly and hard.

Quite apart from the question of sin, it would seem to be in the very nature of love and self-giving to involve some degree of self denial and the inevitable pain of being torn apart within. Love is not possible unless one dies to oneself; there must be self-emptying, a *kenosis*, as St Paul says in reference to Christ. This is why the life of Christ is our model for giving, and for growth towards the perfection of self-offering. Every single moment of his life bears the mark of this unceasing gesture of oblation which defines his Sonship. There is no self-seeking, nothing in him which is not inspired by charity alone. We, too, must try to imitate this by making our lives into an offering, consecrating them to God, as far as we are able, as a continual sacrifice, putting aside the idea that sacrifice must necessarily be painful, disagreeable and negative. It will be, as long as we have not reached perfect love. When love is perfected, blessing and sacrifice coincide, as the passion and resurrection of Christ demonstrate. The offering of ourselves must be made joyfully and is best expressed where grace is at work, turning our lives into a hymn to the goodness of God our Father. When we experience pain and death – which we inevitably will – they are destroyed, transformed into love, and, finally, into a joy which is not of this world.

It is in this context that the Eucharist mediates the power of sacrifice and divinity, offertory and transfiguration. If Christ accepted death, if he agreed to take upon himself all the tragedy of the human condition, to be abandoned, condemned and shamefully mocked, to become the man of sorrows through the pain he endured and the hideous suffering of the cross, it was in order to overcome all these horrors by the glory of his resurrection. It was so that in him and through him, death might lead not to meaninglessness and despair but to life. This is the significance of the work of Christ: the most dreadful suffering, and even death itself, are transfigured by love to become a perfect sacrifice, an offering which opens the way to eternal life. Before Christ death itself, and all the trials, illness, griefs, failures and humiliations which we experience as so many partial deaths throughout our lives, ended in nothingness and despair, or at best in a grim and stoical resignation. With Christ, all these negative and tragic elements take on a new significance; they are turned into positive opportunities to become alive to new depths, to advance in self-denial and love. Within the supreme sacrifice of Christ, everything can become an offering, a gift which will be consumed in the fire of the Spirit, and a spring of life to the Father's glory.

All this is obviously difficult to put into practise straight away since our reaction to suffering is always one of rebellion and despair; but the possibility remains open. The Eucharist is celebrated hundreds of thousands of times a day throughout the world for this one reason: so that through it, human suffering and death might be transfigured, united with the suffering and death of Christ.

The Eucharist as a transfiguring sacrifice

"God became man so that human beings might be made God": this formula provided the main guidelines for all theological reflection in the first centuries. To be sacrificed, to become a sacrifice in Christ and to become divine, are one and the same thing. The Eucharist is the chief means to this deification of humanity in all its reality: its sensuality, its pain or its pleasure. It is not only a question of offering death and suffering in sacrifice, but the whole of human life, its joys and sorrows, death and birth, love and discord, labour, and that immense striving after the conquest and transformation of the world, the fruit of which is symbolised in the bread of the Eucharist. In the Eucharist our humanity in all its entirety, the intelligence which enables us to reflect and create, our freedom, our capacity for love, suffering or happiness, is offered with the humanity of Christ, in it and through it. In the Eucharist the Word of God takes hold of us, clothes us with his Spirit and shapes us after his likeness, so that we come to resemble him perfectly and are made one with him.

All of this can be summarized by saying that in and through the Eucharist, the transfiguration of the whole of humanity is completed, and by emphasising that God does not replace humanity. The human condition remains the same, suffering and death do not disappear, history is not abolished; rather, human beings gradually become God, become divine in the very fabric of their behaviour. Suffering in particular does not disappear; instead it is lit from within, it is transformed and filled with hope, it opens out into newness of life. Similarly, the bread is not suddenly replaced by Christ but becomes, even while it remains bread, the Body of Christ: it takes on a new, richer dimension. We must understand that God does not replace humanity, but rather humanity receives the power to become divine without ceasing to be human, and without being spared anything of the human condition and its tragedy. Sickness, old age, wars and accidents affect us just as much as they do non-Christians, but in Christ they open up the (free) possibility of a way through to resurrection and newness of life.

The Eucharist as the centre of history and the centre of the world

In Eucharistic exposition, the host is seen at the centre of a monstrance made in the form a cross from which radiate shafts of light. The host is thus at the centre of the world, symbolised by the horizontal arm of the cross, and at the point where time meets eternity, symbolised by the vertical arm. God and the world are united in Christ, who is both the human being, born of Mary, and, at the same time, the Word of God, born of the eternal Father. In the bread, we find summarised the whole of human history from the beginnings of time and the slow rise of progress towards the humanisation of nature at the hands of human beings. We find, also, the whole story of God's purpose as creator and saviour, the long series of calls addressed to Israel and, finally, the adventure of the Word of God, who was born into our world, crucified and who rose again in glory. The whole history of salvation is condensed and summarised in this bread. Thus the Eucharist can be seen as the absolute centre of the world and of history. It is the starting point, the alpha, which radiates the power of grace, the power which can bestow divinity and which is destined to transfigure the world. It is also the end point, the omega, the point where history converges, the Body of Christ into which the whole universe is destined to be gathered in that glorious hour when the Son will hand all things over to his Father and when God will be all in all, at the end of time.

The golden rays of the monstrance symbolise this

double movement: on the one hand, they stand for the divine power which radiates out over the world and the cosmos. On the other hand they symbolise the convergence of all that is outward towards a centre, a pole which brings to a focus the progress of humanity, the omega point of history and of the evolution of the cosmos. The Eucharist draws the whole world to itself, and seeks to absorb it all.

The Eucharist as the centre of our interiority

The Eucharist is both a focus and a point of diffusion. It leads us inwards, yet draws us out of ourselves towards a beyond which is found in sacrifice and self-giving. It is both presence and absence. It is presence, in that out of the Eucharist the power of Love shines forth over the whole world. It is absence, in that this thin, almost transparent piece of bread conceals as much as it reveals of the divine presence. That presence is sensed as a call, a gulf drawing all things to itself; a hollow, an infinite absence, an unknowable absolute in which we lose our powers of reason, something beyond all our conception, like the depths of darkness we sense beyond the brightness of the stars. Thus the Eucharist allows us to approach the hiddenmost centre of our interiority which is at the same time the centre of the world. In the Eucharist, our humanity discovers itself to be the temple of God and here, too, we join in the history of the whole human family, and are united to others at their deepest roots, where God gives them being and bestows on them his saving love.

Through the Eucharist we become present to human history and to the tragedy of the world's suffering and death, in the same way as Jesus is present in them, taking them upon himself in love and self-giving and so transforming them into a perfect sacrifice to the Father. In the Eucharist we give sense and meaning to human suffering by seeing it in terms of sacrifice. This can be done with a greater degree of truthfulness the deeper our personal involvement in the sacrifice. Such involvement comes through our own suffering and through a compassion for others which finds its model in Mary.

Each one of us is given a part in the mystery of redeeming compassion according to our own capacity. Personal suffering and hardship alone allow us to enter into the passion of Christ; there is no other way. Unless we have personally experienced suffering we will remain on the outside, more or less spectators however well meaning we may be. But once suffering has done its work of death within us we can, if we truly want to, enter into and share in the sacrifice of Christ and through offering and complete acceptance, transform this suffering into love, and so into a spring of life both for ourselves and for others.

This is the call which radiates from the focal point of the Eucharist. It is a path which leads towards the ultimate beyond, the absorption and consummation of the whole, tragic reality of history in the burning heat of absolute Love, the source and end of all things. This is the call to which the Virgin Mary responds with an unparalleled depth of generosity. A person like Marthe Robin provides us with a concrete example of what it can mean to take upon oneself the anguish and distress of the world and to offer one's whole being as a perfect sacrifice and a total Eucharist. 'The long mass of Marthe Robin' is the title of one of her biographies, a title which is full of significance theologically and which sums up so well the mystery of a totally eucharistic life. Surely our own lives are destined to become Eucharist, offered for the salvation of the world, and our own selves destined to become hosts, given up in sacrifice, springs of life for the whole world! This is the call echoing from the monstrance where the crucified Word is revealed as the unique path which alone leads towards the immeasurable gulf of that absolute Love which, through the Spirit, we are bold to call 'Abba, Father!' Alone with the Alone, our solitude becomes or can become a Eucharist, an offering, a source of redeeming compassion, a spring of life for the world. In the innermost emptiness of our desert, in its most profound desolation flow forth living eucharistic springs which wash away all the anguish, all the pain and all the sin of the world.

Chapter 8
Prayer, the way of interiority

There is a whole philosophy behind this undertaking to journey to the inner kingdom and to the dwelling place of God at the depths of the heart. The monks of the hesychastic tradition frequently use an expression which may at first seem curious: 'To descend with the mind into the heart.' They are simply attempting to suggest an ideal of unification, a restoration of humanity to its original unity, a rediscovery of the deep springs of being and life which flow up within it through the creating and re-creating power of God.

The quest for peace, the search for the springs of true life, the desire to achieve a quality and depth of existence which will make us fully human, not just outwardly through the conquest and possession of a world of illusion, but inwardly, in the silence and peace which we glimpse or experience personally in rare, brief moments: these are ideals shared by many philosophies and religions apart from Christianity. The desire to leave behind the inconstancy and deceit of the superficial world in order to discover the centre of all truth, truth itself, the truth of creation; the desire to turn away from the folly of outward busyness in order to journey deep into the only reality which has real weight and value; to turn one's back on the din of a civilisation which destroys humanity, in order to reach that silence which unites the whole world in Love: this, it seems, forms the heart of an undertaking which is typically monastic and to which we might give the very broad name 'prayer'.

What does prayer mean for the Christian, and what is implied by that most difficult concept 'contemplation' or the contemplative life? Surely it is the capacity to be attentive to the very essence of things, discerned within ourselves and at the heart of all reality! To see in a contemplative way means to look with penetrating eyes, with a pure and peaceful gaze which reaches the truth, the ultimate essence of beings and persons. For those of us who are Christians this essence takes the form of a face, the face of the Word of God. Our one task is to find a way to approach the mystery of God, the creator and saviour who gives himself to us in and through all things, and in ourselves first of all.

Christian interiority

In the Gospel, Christ tells us insistently that the kingdom of God is within us. It is not a kingdom which can be established through power and conquest or by means of political organisation; it comes instead through the conversion and transformation of the human heart. Hearts which are burdened by sin and filled with violence and pride can be cleansed and illumined by the Holy Spirit and so become temples of the living God. At the heart of the good news which the Gospel announces to the world is the promise of the Spirit, given to us by the Father through his beloved Son. If we are living out the Gospel we will be aware of the wonderful gift of the Spirit within us, giving us peace, making us kind and forgiving towards one another, helping us to maintain a deep inner joy even in the most difficult of circumstances, destroying our prejudices and making us as simple, loving and innocent as children. Once cleansed by the exacting demands of ascetic discipline, our prayer and contemplation will lead us to be more and more attentive to the extraordinary treasures which we carry within us: the treasures of peace, goodness and beauty, treasures found in a face.

For the Absolute which we discover in our hearts and at the depths of all reality is not some infinite, unknowable gulf, nor a totality which would have no meaning for us, even if we should recognise it as the fullness of all that is. No, the Absolute takes the form of a face. It has the face of the Word of God, the creator and saviour whose transcendence was made manifest to the world in Jesus of Nazareth. Here we are at the heart of the Christian revelation: the Absolute which we approach in contemplative prayer has a face, or rather it is a face, or love, or a person. These are the words which can most surely direct our minds towards the Beyond which instinct tells us is both the source and ultimate fulfilment of the present of our daily lives as well as of the future of history and the cosmos.

A vital breath

Within the narrow confines of our world of pleasure and pain, ambition and failure, love and grief, desire and despair, enchantment and disgust, futile joy and vague sadness, a secret voice of calling can be heard. At first faint, like the murmur of a song, it becomes a symphonic hymn. Hope is made alive; another world, another truth, another light can be glimpsed through the cracks in the suffocating, tragic, meaningless prison of our world: prayer.

Each human heart, in its unique mystery as a personality created in the image of God, is the potential setting for the miracle of this compelling call to light and life, to the love which can bring salvation and to a freely given creative force of peace and beauty. Happy are those who allow this call to well up inside them and so fill them that their whole being echoes with beseeching and praise. But these same people can instead let the trap-door of despair and rebellion, shameful desires and petty dislikes, close over their heads. Having glimpsed light through a crack in the prison wall of this narrow world, they can once again choose enslavement to suffocating pride and the selfish folly which always demands its own way. Prayer is silenced, the song of freedom is stifled and the dreary noises of sadness, anger, scorn and futile ambition start up again with renewed strength. The unending spiral of evil thoughts make them prisoners once more of the powers of darkness. Hell again casts its suffocating shadow over a heart into which the Spirit of God had begun to breathe true freedom. When prayer dies, we die with it.

A breath from outside us

Prayer is a gift of the Spirit. Those who are imprisoned in the narrow confines of their sin and held captive by the powers of darkness, can never think of raising their eyes to God and calling on the love and forgiveness of the Almighty unless it is given them to do so. It is the Spirit of God who enlightens and arouses our desire. Because we are completely free we can deny the Spirit and choose death; but we can also surrender to it and let it hold us more and more firmly. And what is the Spirit saying within us? "Abba, Father!" (Rom 8:15). This one cry expresses the whole mystery of our destiny: we have wandered far from the source of our creation and are making our way back along a road which leads through hardship and death to new life as children of God and to an eternity which has already begun.

'Abba, Father!' is the cry which gradually shapes us as children of God, one with the Son, eternally offered to the Father. It is a song which echoes ever more powerfully in the depths of our soul. It can be filled with distress, a cry for help from the pit of anguish and grief into which our lives have thrown us, or it can express our trust in the supreme goodness of a Father who watches over us and by whom even the hairs of our head are numbered.

'Abba, Father!' is a cry of entreaty arising in the farthest parts of the earth out of the tremendous pain of a human family torn apart by hatred and overwhelmed by hideous suffering. As members of the human family, our voices too rise in solidarity. All who pray, who are 'little brothers of all' in Charles de Foucauld's words, who enfold in love those who are united to them in the huge, Mystical Body of Christ, are, through the cry of 'Abba, Father!" making intercession in a solidarity which aims to make them one with all people. It is the prayer of those whose hearts have been enlarged by trials until they are able to contain the enormous suffering of humanity.

'Abba, Father!' is the inner song of all contemplatives who take upon themselves in love all the suffering of the world and offer it to the Father, appealing to his mercy, to the 'bowels of his compassion' as the Bible puts it. It is the song of pleading which the Spirit arouses in the hearts of those whose lives are lived in such total solidarity that they have become nothing other than a sacrifice of intercession.

'Abba, Father!' is an expression of the total assent which the Spirit of Christ awakens in the human soul. It voices the surrender of the human heart to the wisdom of the Father who watches over the world and who governs each detail of our lives with love, so that at all times, in wonder, trust and humility, we can be in communion with that wisdom which is far greater than our own. It also indicates our willing assent to do all that the Father asks of us for the salvation of the world: to proclaim the Gospel, to overcome the evil within us, and to bring a little joy, kindness and beauty to those who are crushed by hopelessness or contempt. The Spirit reveals to us the mystery hidden in God from before the world began, the mystery of the Father who leads back his lost creatures and gives us our own place in the vast enterprise of history.

Finally, the cry 'Abba, Father!' captures the exultant praise of the prodigal child who rediscovers the love, peace and splendour of its father's home at the heart of a radiantly beautiful creation which suddenly reflects, as in a mirror, the face of inaccessible silence.

Contemplation

The Spirit enables us to see. Contemplation means looking in order to see. It does not involve spectacular and wonderful visions, but rather the mercy and the loving power of God at work in the world and in the human heart. Through the eyes of historians and journalists we are only able to see events at a very superficial level; we are shown only what can be filmed or recorded. Such techniques show just how shallow this vision is, in which history becomes little more than pictures on a vast screen, mostly tragic and inevitably absurd, an incoherent and dramatic play of shadows empty of any substance and meaning. In contrast, the contemplative vision penetrates to the depths of events, bringing to light the meaning behind them and investing them with an eternal significance. They take on the invisible dimension of good or evil, of consent or refusal. They are seen in terms of the furtherance of the kingdom or its hindrance, of faces which are destined for death or for life, or, as St John says, in terms of a judgement which ensures either the victory of light over darkness or its defeat.

Every event, whether a war or a human-made disaster, a scientific discovery or the creation of a work of art, a political election or a strike, has an eternal dimension in that it indicates a yes or a no addressed to God by humanity. Through these events, human beings draw nearer to God and journey towards truth, peace and love, or, instead, turn aside to be tragically lost in the darkness of denial.

The contemplative vision penetrates to the very secret of creation to discover its meaning in the cross of Christ. The cross is the true centre of history and all things are ordered in relation to it. It is the point where earth and heaven meet; in it and through it, the journey of each civilisation, each nation and each one of us in our individual destiny comes to an end in the kingdom of God. In it and through it the whole of human reality is caught up into the light of the Spirit, or else remains doomed to darkness and death. The cross is indeed the key to the mystery of creation, enabling us to see all things even as God sees them. It is the supreme object of our contemplation and ever present to it and, in particular, it sheds the light of meaning on the mystery of our life and personality.

Goodness, mercy and wonder

Prayer enables us to see the world with new eyes, with the eyes of contemplation which focus not on the evil in creation but on the light. "If your eye is healthy, your whole body will be full of light" (Mt 6:22). Only the charity which comes from God is able to cleanse our minds, sharpen our intuition and tune our hearing and our spiritual senses, allowing them to be filled with wonder at the splendours brought about by God's grace at work in the world. Evil people see only evil around them; their bitter hopelessness, their hatred and criticism merely serve to project the deep shadows of their inner world onto the world outside. Innocence alone is capable of discerning innocence and feeling wonder. The grace of God and the redemption brought by Christ are not just empty phrases. There are great treasures of holiness, wonderful works of charity and generous springs of creativity both inside and outside the Church. There is no denying that humanity is sinful and that dreadful things do happen. But life is stronger than death and where sin is present, there grace is present in greater measure; the resurrection of Jesus never ceases to bring about this marvellous passage from death to life, from despair to fullness of joy, from the curse of sin to the eternal, eucharistic blessing in which is expressed the heart of the good news brought to the world by the Word of God.

Only if we are cleansed by the light of the Spirit can we approach the reality which alone is true, divine and eternal. Only the innocent eyes of a child of the kingdom can see of their own accord with sufficient depth and clarity to perceive, beneath the accumulation of sin, the wonderful, future face of humanity which is slowly emerging in the splendour of the risen Christ. The pessimism which results from anguish is in the end merely superficial. The truth, in contrast, is "hidden from the wise and intelligent, but revealed to infants" (Mt 11:25), to those with a purity of vision, a generosity of love, and a simplicity of heart which place them at the level of the deepest realities of God's love, given in Jesus for the salvation of the world.

A heart of flame

St John saw Christ's heart pierced by a spear, pouring out water and blood to bring life to the world. St Margaret Mary received the gift of a heart radiant with light, and it was Charles de Foucauld, the 'little brother of all', who first drew the image, now reproduced so often, of a cross implanted in a heart. It was his banner, a symbol of the life he sought to live.

At the centre of the world is the heart of the Word of God, creator and saviour. It is a heart which pours out a never-ending stream of life, in which and through which this world is transformed. This heart is the starting point of a transfiguring flood which will lead matter, subject as it is to the rigid laws of science, to surrender once again to the freedom of the spirit. Above all, it will turn our humanity, at present torn apart by the violence of sin and the savage, animal instincts which we still retain, into a shining icon, a mystical face or body in which the Spirit of God will set forth his marvellous gifts.

Our own hearts are destined to beat to the same rhythm as the heart of the world. They are to receive the same eucharistic blood and spread forth the same life which will shatter from within the pitiless rigidity of a world which is subject to the violence of the strong and which makes riches and power its idols. Interiority is simply another name for the depths of the human heart where the power of the Spirit takes root. The power of the Spirit alone is able to shake and split apart the formidable cohesion of the oppressive universe of sin, a universe in which humanity is held captive by the sordid lure of wealth, the pride which deludes us into an infatuation with knowledge and the deceitful illusions of power. Dangerous and without remorse, wealth, power and knowledge are the commonly named idols worshipped by the modern world, just as they have always been, which are responsible for the creation of the prison in which humanity lives. These idols are no more than the glitter of deceptive appearances, illusions expertly conjured up by the Prince of this world.

"The tax-collectors and the prostitutes are going into the kingdom of God ahead of you" (Mt 21:31). They are the poor ones who have no wealth, no culture, no influence, and whose hearts are not closed, hardened or corrupted by idolatry. The poor of the Gospel are free to welcome the good news of liberation, love and the advent of another world. The cry 'Abba, Father!' arises spontaneously in the hearts of such *poverellos* as Francis of Assisi, turning them into glowing fires, furnaces of transfiguration for the world.

Interiority and history

As humanity makes huge efforts to rise towards the light, a whisper of breath finds its way through the various forms of religious life, from its most primitive manifestations in pre-history to its most advanced, purified and mystical states. It is a powerful force which works cautiously and ambiguously, which is sometimes deformed and perverted, but which reaches its full glory and purity in Christianity. The Spirit of God, the divine breath, gradually makes its dwelling within a humanity made mature through a long and often painful process of growth and leads it on the long road towards the high peaks of light to which the Father draws it.

Prayer is the breath of humanity as it journeys on its way. It is prayer which arouses and gives expression to our tireless search for that which is beyond us. Prayer is the ceaseless questioning and the tentative response repeated at varying depths by each successive generation and civilisation. Only human beings are capable of asking such "damned big questions" (Chestov), they alone seek to understand the meaning of the world and of their own lives, they alone feel the irresistible call to transcendence which hints at the existence of a Truth capable of satisfying their anguished searching. Why death, why love and evil and hatred? The spirit within us is awake and watchful, aspiring through the present after that which is beyond. This aspiration is both a cry of pain and a cry of hope.

Prayer can never in fact be thought of, as people often tend to, merely in terms of an easy approach to the sublime, a pious daydream, a flight of contemplation or a waft of pleasant feelings, whether maudlin or ecstatic. Prayer is essentially a cry which seeks to pierce through the tragic weight of history to give it meaning and open the way to hope. Prayer which rises from the depths of the heart, from the interiority which makes humanity free, seeks to enfold and transfigure history. A life rooted in concrete reality, like that lived by the people of God, is absolutely essential if Christian contemplation, even in its most elevated and ecstatic form, is to bear its weight of earth and blood. Our prayer can be no different from the prayer of the crucified God-made-man, the disfigured, transfigured man whose passion and resurrection determine our path, flooding it with the brilliance of their light as together we all live out the same adventure.

What does it mean to pray? It means allowing the hope which comes from outside us to emerge from the depths of our hearts; it means listening to a song of silence which, at first barely audible, gradually becomes a symphony in which the strident discords of the infinite diversity of notes which make up our human-divine reality are at last resolved in a vast, paradoxical silence where all things disappear and at the same time find their ultimate fulfilment; it means allowing wonder and tenderness for each gleam of beauty found in the heart of creation and in every face to well up inside us and overflow in praise and glory; it means letting the wound of compassion bleed for every experience of distress; it means allowing our eyes to weep for every hurt and our lips to groan at each act of violence; it means standing at the centre of the world where in the deep, primordial silence our human adventure takes flight and completes its journey back into the fullness of the Father. It was Therese of the Child Jesus who expressed a desire to be the love at the heart of the Church.

Towards the inner kingdom

We can only reach the centre of the world, or the world beyond this world – the spatial imagery is of little importance – by a willingness to strip away 'that which is not', in order to lose ourselves completely in the one whose name is "I am" (Ex 3:14). The path held out by the Gospel is one which descends in humility towards the living springs; which confronts us with the poverty of nothingness and death, that the divine gleam of the "treasure in clay jars" (2 Cor 4:7) might be revealed once the jar of clay is broken. It is a path which descends further still towards the depths of life and being, tearing us away from the superficiality of false riches and the deceptive wisdom of this world. To follow this path means trampling to dust the superficial, cumbersome self, swollen with pride, so that the child of the Gospel can be born in the miraculous waters of Baptism which flow in the depth of the heart. This is the path which leads to the inner kingdom which, once again, is no other than the kingdom which will come at the end of time when Christ has gathered all things to himself, to offer them to the Father in a final liturgy, a final prayer.